A Time and a Place

The ELP Story

Laura Shenton

A Time and a Place

The ELP Story

Laura Shenton

WP
WYMER
PUBLISHING
Bedford, England

First published in 2022 by Wymer Publishing
Bedford, England www.wymerpublishing.co.uk Tel: 01234 326691
Wymer Publishing is a trading name of Wymer (UK) Ltd

Copyright © 2022 Laura Shenton / Wymer Publishing.

Print edition (fully illustrated): **ISBN: 978-1-915246-14-1**

Edited by Jerry Bloom.

The Author hereby asserts her rights to be identified
as the author of this work in accordance with sections
77 to 78 of the Copyright, Designs & Patents Act 1988.

All rights reserved. No part of this publication may be
reproduced or transmitted in any form or by any means,
electronic or mechanical, including photocopying, or any
information storage and retrieval system, without written
permission from the publisher.

This publication is sold subject to the condition that it shall not,
by way of trade or otherwise, be lent, re-sold, hired out or
otherwise circulated without the publishers' prior consent in any
form of binding or cover other than that in which it is published
and without a similar condition including this condition
being imposed on the subsequent purchaser.

eBook formatting by Coinlea.
Printed and bound in Great Britain by
CMP, Dorset.

A catalogue record for this book is available from the British Library.

Typeset/Design by Andy Bishop / 1016 Sarpsborg
Cover design by 1016 Sarpsborg.

Contents

Preface   7

1. From The Beginning   9

2. From The Flight Of The Seagull   27

3. People Are Stirred   35

4. I've Seen Paupers As Kings   51

5. You Could Be Anything   65

6. Everything You've Ever Dreamed   87

7. I'm Moving Out Of Here   109

8. Learning To Fly   119

9. Every Day I See A New Cloud Coming   125

10. A Legend   137

Discography   141

Tour Dates   146

"To me, there's soul in everything we've ever played. I just think it's a little harder to recognise because of its complexity sometimes. I'm sure you can get lost in some of our music, especially on first hearing. I doubt if you can pick up on the soul first time through, but it's there all the same."

- Greg Lake, speaking to *New Musical Express* in March 1973

Preface

In one of my other books on Emerson, Lake and Palmer (*Pictures At An Exhibition – In-Depth*, also by Wymer Publishing), to an extent, the narrative is driven by my own opinion of the music. That is to say that I consider *Pictures At An Exhibition* to be something of an underdog album in ELP's discography; the band themselves were unsure as to whether they wanted it to be released and, back in the day, live releases by any band were considered to be something of a throwaway and were sold at a lower price point (they did cost less to make than a studio album, but still).

In holding that opinion, inevitably, the narrative of that book is centred on all of the positive things that I wanted to bring to light about the album. Sure, factual information is included in abundance, but it is often considered through the lens of my own bias. With this book here, you will find that I have steered clear of putting my own opinion at the essence of the narrative. The reason for this is that although there are already a few books out there on ELP, there are not so many of them that the facts surrounding the band are as readily available to readers as say, material on The Beatles, Elvis, or Bob Dylan.

There is still so much solid fact about ELP that has yet to be collated and preserved in book form that, in view of the existing literature so far, it makes sense with this book to take the opportunity to communicate factually rather than with the motive to add my own reviews and opinions of ELP's music, achievements, and indeed, challenges.

As part of the latter, throughout this book, you will find that I've quoted liberally from a wide range of vintage resources. The purpose of this is to communicate what was happening for ELP *at the time*. For instance, with the advantage of hindsight, it would be all too easy to assume that success was going to be a given for ELP. There were certainly times though, where that wouldn't have felt like the case for the band — back when they were actively living those moments, with no idea what the future would bring. In the early seventies, who could have predicted that towards the end of the decade, progressive rock would have reached a point of — for many — tedium? And indeed, when John Peel slated ELP as "a complete waste of time, talent and electricity", who could have guessed that the band would go on to prove him significantly wrong? (and then some!).

I have had no affiliation with ELP, or with any of their associates. This book is the product of research that has been undertaken with no bias other than the fact that clearly, I like the band and want to participate in the preservation of their fascinating legacy. I won't be offering a speculative exploration into the interpersonal dynamics within the band. With all but one of the members having passed away, I don't feel that it would be fair to do so.

More than that though, as much as any fan may have wanted to be a fly on the wall and privy to this kind of thing at the time, the fact is that nobody really was. And therefore, who really would have the right to state strands of gossip about any band arguments as fact? For what it's worth, in both of their autobiographies, both Emerson and Lake had moments where they didn't speak particularly favourably about each other, often stating that the future of ELP looked tentative on many occasions throughout even the most successful times of their tenure. Overall though, it comes across that the band had a constructive rapport and knew that they worked well together, as is evidenced in their phenomenal musical output.

This book is going to give you not only a nostalgia trip, but a wealth of information about Emerson, Lake and Palmer's albums and tours, the motives and outcomes behind them, and indeed, what it means to be able to appreciate such an impressive legacy today.

1.
From The Beginning

Due to the vast extent of skill and overall musicianship in Emerson, Lake and Palmer's music, their work has been, understandably, taken as seriously as it clearly demands. It has often been the case though, that due to the way in which the band blended classical and rock influences together, labels such as "pompous", "indulgent" and "overly serious" were sometimes directed at them in considerable abundance. It would be easy to overlook how, at the heart of it, ELP was not only a gregarious, outgoing and innovative band, but a fun and entertaining one too.

In January 1972, a local American newspaper commented on the band's audience appeal; "Emerson, Lake and Palmer's volume may not caress sensitive eardrums, but they are the most musical of the loud, hard groups. Well-developed with shifting textures and moods, ELP's music is both melodic and exciting. Influenced by jazz and classical music as well as rock, Keith Emerson on keyboard dominates this British trio. They are one of the few groups to use a Moog synthesiser, an electric instrument capable of producing an infinite variety of sounds. The musicianship of Emerson, bassist and vocalist Greg Lake, and drummer Carl Palmer attracts slightly older, more sophisticated enthusiasts, but their showmanship still holds the attraction of younger fans. Outfitted in dripping fringes and flashy fabrics, Emerson rocks the organ back and forth, leaps over it, hurls knives into the keys and hauls the whole instrument on his back, like Atlas holding up the world. At the finish, he lies on the floor, pulls the organ down on top of him and plays from that position. What kid could resist jumping out of his seat and screaming for more of such a spectacle?"

Another journalist commented the same year; "One other delightful aspect of Emerson, Lake and Palmer is their sense of humour. If you ever get to the point where you suspect that they might be getting a bit pretentious, you suddenly find yourself singing 'Mama's little baby got shortenin', shortenin'". I don't know if Emerson, Lake and Palmer are just paving their own way or pointing out the direction for much of rock's future. When they're not indulging in crowd-pleasing showmanship, the music is extraordinarily demanding and challenging to the listener. Emerson, Lake and Palmer have a style that's unique, and music that's worthy of anyone interested in music and its directions."

When ELP formed in 1970, it was at a time when the music industry and fans alike, both sides of the Atlantic, were wondering what, if anything, was going to take the baton and run with it at the tale-end of The Beatles' most fruitful days. It was at that time that Keith Emerson, Greg Lake and Carl Palmer were, despite what they had achieved in their individual careers previously, still young men — relatively at the start of their careers and raring to go and then some.

Unemployment amongst men of their generation was uncommon. Expected to be self-reliant — and often breadwinners for a family unit — they could expect to get a job working for a local company upon leaving school. It was worlds away from the fun and excitement that the young people of the fifties and sixties perhaps aspired to though. With the fifties had come the emergence of youth culture; the idea of a teenager was not only a sociological phenomenon, but a group of people whom something could be marketed to — something engrained in ideals of entertainment and even, identity. Music was the perfect outlet, and indeed, vehicle for such phenomenon.

Whilst the sixties carried ideals of liberal use of creativity in all areas of the arts, the commerciality of popular music continued to thrive. On the one hand, The Beatles had levels of success that saw the marketing formula used in their favour, used again and again for many groups for decades to come. On the other, there were groups considered more experimental, delving into sounds that would be liberally labelled as acid jazz and associated with the likes of hippies and the weird and wonderful range of recreational drugs that came with the whole scene. And indeed, sometimes the two aesthetics came together, as was the case on The Beatles' more psychedelically inspired 1967 album, *Sgt Pepper's Lonely Hearts Club Band*. Of course, many other genres of popular music were thriving around that time but commercially, there remained a large question mark over what would next strike a chord with the record-buying public.

When the young Keith Emerson, Greg Lake and Carl Palmer found themselves on the wild ride of being heralded as the new supergroup towards the end of 1970, they certainly weren't a trio of classically trained musicians who had just turned up with silver spoons in their mouths assuming that they would, as has so often been said in the music industry, "make it". "They seemed to think we'd had it easy," said Lake. "I'd like to meet anyone who thinks *I've* had it easy, for a start. I've worked like bloody hell in this business for years, man, and I've starved. I've slept in vans and all the rest of it. At the moment, I couldn't go out and buy a bloody Ford! That's how rich *I* am!"

Endearingly, in a very early interview of the band (it was filmed and not only do they look so young in it, but there is something of an innocence in their answers and how they mostly avoid eye contact with the only camera there), they answered questions about their hobbies and what they would probably be doing if it wasn't for their respective jobs in the band. Each of their responses to the question about their hobbies was said in a tone that makes the footage somewhat amusing to watch. It is that of three young men who, in southern British accents not too different to those which feature in *Spinal Tap*, don't really seem too sure as to why the cameraman is asking them pop-quiz-style questions.

> Lake: "I really haven't ever had time to think about hobbies — working all the time, all the time."

> Palmer: "Hobbies? Driving, I quite like driving, so I just bought a car. I haven't got many hobbies really."

> Emerson: "I don't really have another hobby. I used to have a hobby in photography, and fishing, but no, I've only got time to devote my whole life to music."

Each musician was asked what they would be doing if not for being in the band. Their responses speak volumes about who ELP were at the start of their career:

> Palmer: "I don't know really. I've never really been to work, you see. I really just don't know. That's sort of impossible to ask. I'm a musician and that's how I'd like it to stay really. I was a schoolboy before, because I've never been to work."

> Lake: "I probably wouldn't choose a job, I'd commit suicide."

> Emerson: "I couldn't imagine doing anything else."

With that in mind, what was the background of the three individuals who made up the vital nucleus of Emerson, Lake and Palmer?

****

Keith Noel Emerson was born on 2nd November 1944 in Todmorden, West Yorkshire, to a family who had been evacuated from the south of England during the Second World War. When they returned south and settled in Goring-by-Sea in West Sussex, Emerson attended West Tarring School. Although Emerson's mother wasn't musical, his father played the piano. By the age of eight, Emerson was supported by his parents to attend piano lessons from local tutors. His tuition included how to read music and although emphasis was placed on Western classical music as part of his studies, it wasn't long before he started to develop his own style based on jazz and rock music.

Emerson didn't own a record player but upon listening to the radio, he found that Floyd Cramer's 1961 slip-note style 'On The Rebound' resonated with him, as well as the work of Dudley Moore.

In many ways, Emerson was a self-starter when it came to his early music education. He studied the sheet music of Dave Brubeck and George Shearing and learnt about jazz piano from books.

The young Emerson's piano lessons had been basic-level ones with a local elderly woman. "That lasted for about, say, four or five years," he recalled. "What came out of that was that I could read music, and I could play, and I understood the theory. After that I taught myself. Now, I didn't study harmony and composition and counterpoint, or all that sort of thing. I bought books, read about whatever I wanted to do. When I started writing fugues, I bought a book on how a fugue is constructed. It's constructed quite mathematically really and I just made various notes studying how the Bach flowed. I based my fugues around that way."

"I started playing piano by ear, and my parents thought, 'Ah, he's got a gift for this'. And from that moment I hated it: it was scales and it was playing these classical pieces. I had a love of jazz when I was a teenager, and I think Brubeck was a great influence, and I read one of his liner notes — he and Paul Desmond used a lot of counterpoint within their jazz improvisation. I thought 'That's interesting'. So I went back and dug out my old music books — particularly Bach — and I started incorporating those into my piano solos."

"You can't be taught to play music, you have to be born to play it," he said. "Ever since the age of two I was going round the house making songs up. There was a piano in the house and I learned to play by ear. My father was musical and that's where it came from. I didn't read music so later I taught myself to. Music schools are good, but they have rules in music and you can't have rules in music... When you're taught you have to play what the composer wrote, you're not allowed to improvise — whereas in a lot of cases the composer wrote improvisationally. Worked-out solos are okay, but there's always that spark of surprise when you do something spontaneous, you can't recreate that."

Emerson's sources of inspiration were diverse. He listened to boogie-woogie, and to country-style pianists including Joe "Mr Piano" Henderson, Russ Conway and Winifred Atwell. Emerson later said of himself: "I was a very serious child. I used to walk around with Beethoven sonatas under my arm. However, I was very good at avoiding being beaten up by the bullies. That was because I could also play Jerry Lee Lewis and Little Richard songs. So, they thought I was kind of cool and left me alone."

Emerson's interest in the Hammond organ was ignited after hearing jazz organist Jack McDuff perform 'Rock Candy' — so much so that the Hammond became his instrument of choice in the late 1960s. He rented his first Hammond organ at the age of around fifteen or sixteen. It was an L-100 model.

Initially, Emerson functioned on the basis that music would be a hobby on the side. He played the piano in pubs whilst working at Lloyds Bank during the day. This wasn't to last though. Music became more and more prevalent in how he spent his time and Emerson was fired from his job at the bank.

It was whilst he was performing in the Worthing area that Emerson received an offer to join his first professional band, The T-Bones. They were the backing group of blues singer Gary Farr. The T-Bones toured the UK and France before they all went their separate ways. It was after this that Emerson joined a band called The V.I.P.'s. In 1967 though, the connections that Emerson had made with The T-Bones would come back to the fore, and fantastically so too. With Lee Jackson, who he had worked with in The T-Bones, Emerson formed a new group: The Nice, after soul singer P.P. Arnold had asked him to form a backing band. The other members were David O'List and Ian Hague.

Ultimately, Hague was replaced by Brian Davison. Following the band's commercial success with an instrumental rearrangement of Leonard Bernstein's 'America', O'List left the line-up and the remaining trio soon acquired an intense following on the basis of their live performances. The group had a solid foundation in Emerson's Hammond organ showmanship as well as from his theatrical use of the instrument. Their bold rearrangements of classical music themes have often been described by some as "symphonic rock".

In July 1967, whilst taking note of his "tremendous technique", *Melody Maker* opined of Emerson's contribution to The Nice; "He uses ideas from his classical training and turns them into wild, organ-shaking solos."

Ever keen to add to the visual aspect of his performance, Emerson used his Hammond L-100 organ aggressively — sometimes far beyond what was needed for music, but nevertheless, iconically. He would hit it, beat it with a whip, push it over, ride it across the stage like a horse, play with it lying on top of him, and wedge knives into the keyboard. As much as some of Emerson's actions were very much for show, some of them also produced musical sound effects. Hitting the organ caused it to make sounds that were similar to those of explosions. Turning the organ over resulted in feedback. The knives held down keys and provided the scope for notes to be generously sustained. As a showman, Emerson's appetite for destruction predates many of his peers in the field of rock music.

Unsurprisingly, Emerson was starting to become well known for not only his work with The Nice, but for his work outside of the group. In 1969, he participated in the Music From Free Creek supersession project. It included big names such as Eric Clapton and Jeff Beck. For the session, Emerson performed with drummer Mitch Mitchell and bassist Chuck Rainey. The group covered, among other tunes, the Eddie Harris instrumental 'Freedom Jazz Dance'.

It was in a record shop where Emerson had first heard a Moog. The shop owner played Walter Carlos' *Switched-On Bach* for him. Emerson said of his response at the time; "My God that's incredible, what is that played on?" The owner then showed him the album cover. "So I said, 'What is that?' And he said, 'That's the Moog synthesiser.' My first impression was that it looked a bit like electronic skiffle."

Entranced by the instrument, Emerson borrowed Mike Vickers' Moog for an upcoming Nice concert with the Royal Philharmonic Orchestra at London's Royal Festival Hall. Vickers helped patch the Moog. The concert was a success. Emerson's performance of 'Also Sprach Zarathustra' (a composition most famous for its use in the 1968 film *2001: A Space Odyssey*) was met with much critical acclaim. Emerson later recalled how much the concert made him realise that the Moog was the instrument for him; "I thought, 'this was great. I've got to have one of these'."

****

Greg Lake was born on 10th November 1947 in the Parkstone area of Poole in Dorset. His father, Harry, was an engineer, and his mother, Pearl, was a

From The Beginning

housewife. Lake grew up in Oakdale. He recalled of his childhood that he was "born in an asbestos prefab housing unit" into a "very poor" family where he experienced several cold winters at home. Equally though, Lake spoke highly of his parents for sending him money and food in the days when he was a struggling musician at the start of his career. Overall, Lake asserted that he had a happy upbringing.

It was upon buying Little Richard's 'Lucille' in 1957 that Lake first got into rock 'n' roll music. By the age of twelve, he first learned to play the guitar and it was with even a fundamental knowledge of the instrument that he composed his first song, 'Lucky Man'. He committed it to memory and didn't write it down.

Lake's mother played the piano and in wanting to encourage her son, she got him a second-hand guitar. Lake had lessons with Don Strike, who had a shop in Westbourne. As well as how to read music and exercises based on violin pieces by Niccolò Paganini, Strike taught Lake "these awful Bert Weedon things". Although Lake engaged more with the pop tunes from the 1930s that Strike encouraged him to play, it wasn't much longer than a year after that Lake stopped having lessons with Strike because he wanted to play music that the teacher was keen to discourage — songs by The Shadows. As Lake's journey with the guitar continued, his second was a pink Fender Stratocaster.

Lake went to Oakdale Junior School and then Henry Harbin Secondary Modern School, which he left in either 1963 or 1964. He went straight to work in a job where he was required to load and unload cargo at the Poole docks. He also worked as a draughtsman for a short period. It wasn't long after that Lake made the decision to become a full-time musician — he was seventeen by that point.

Lake's first band was a group by the name of Unit Four. He contributed guitar and vocals. They played cover songs. When they split up in 1965, Lake and the band's bassist, Dave Genes, formed another covers group called The Time Checks. They remained together until 1966. It was after this that Lake then became a member of The Shame. He is featured on their single, 'Don't Go Away Little Girl'. The song was written by Janis Ian.

Whilst in Carlisle for a gig, Lake contracted pneumonia. He continued to perform on stage but his band mates refused to drive back home that night. As a result, he "woke up blue" from having had no other choice but to sleep in the van. He recalled, "When we got home I was nearly dead... That was probably the worst I went through."

After a brief stint in The Shy Limbs, by 1968, Lake was in a band called The Gods. Based in Hatfield, he described his experience of being in the group as "a very poor training college". Despite this, they did manage to secure a residency at the Marquee Club in London. Unhappy with the creative direction the band was taking, Lake left them in 1968, just as they were to enter the recording studio! Their keyboard player Ken Hensley later confessed that Lake "was far too talented to be kept in the background".

Robert Fripp was also from Dorset and had also had guitar lessons with Don Strike. Fripp had seen Lake perform in Poole when he was in Unit Four. Fripp and Lake first began playing guitar together when Fripp was asked to be a roadie for a gig at Ventnor in the Isle of Wight. When no audience turned up, the duo began jamming and playing songs that they had both learnt in their lessons with Strike.

Fripp formed King Crimson when his previous group, Giles, Giles and Fripp failed to gain any traction commercially. On top of this, their record company had already suggested getting a proper lead singer. In response, Fripp chose Lake for the role of vocalist. He asked him to play bass instead of guitar on the basis that it eliminated the need to find a bass player for the group. Lake had predominantly been a guitarist for eleven years and the personnel dilemma handed to him by King Crimson was such that it was his first time to play bass.

Although Peter Sinfield was the lyricist for King Crimson, Lake had some involvement in the process when it came to the writing for the band's debut album, *In The Court Of The Crimson King*. Lake also produced the album as a result of their originally contracted producer, Tony Clarke, walking out midway through the project. When the album came out in October 1969, it was met with both critical acclaim and commercial success. Lake said, "There was this huge wave of response. The audiences were really into us because we were an underground thing — the critics loved us because we offered something fresh." Respectably, the album got to number five in the UK and to number twenty-eight on the Billboard 200 chart.

King Crimson supported their debut album with tours of the UK and the US. Some of the shows featured The Nice as the opening act. It was whilst in the US that Lake struck up a friendship with Nice keyboard player Keith Emerson. They both had similar musical interests in common and it was through this that they began to consider the benefits of forming a new group together.

King Crimson returned to the UK in early 1970. Lake agreed to sing on the band's second album, *In The Wake Of Poseidon*, as well as to appear on *Top Of The Pops* with them, to perform the song 'Cat Food' (notably though, he didn't sing on the single's B-side, 'Groon'). Really,

From The Beginning

it could be considered that Lake was doing Robert Fripp a favour; the then-unknown Elton John had been booked to sing on the *In The Wake Of Poseidon* recording sessions. At the last minute though, Fripp had second thoughts and then cancelled the booking. Lake agreed to step in on the condition that he would be given King Crimson's PA equipment in return. He ended up contributing to all but one of the album's vocal tracks, 'Cadence And Cascade', which was sung by Fripp's old schoolfriend and teenage bandmate, Gordon Haskell.

****

Carl Frederick Kendall Palmer was born on 20th March 1950. He began taking drum lessons as a young boy. He recalled; "I saw a film with Sal Mineo, the film was called *Drum Crazy*. He really captured the image of a drummer for me. I saw that film and that was it really; I knew I didn't want to be a doctor."

Palmer formed his first band with others from the Midlands area; they initially named themselves The King Bees but soon changed their name to The Craig. In 1966, they made their first record. The A-side was a song called 'I Must Be Mad' and on the B-side was 'Suspense'. It was produced by Larry Page. Palmer also started doing session work. He played on the song, 'Love Light', for a band from Liverpool, The Chants. Palmer was invited to join Chris Farlowe and The Thunderbirds later that year.

Palmer then joined The Crazy World Of Arthur Brown, who had already had their famous hit, 'Fire'. Original drummer, Drachen Theaker, played on that track and indeed on their eponymous album. When Theaker suddenly left The Crazy World Of Arthur Brown partway through a tour of the US in 1969, Palmer was quickly brought in as a replacement but he soon became a permanent member of the band.

It didn't last for long though; the keyboard player of the band, Vincent Crane, left at the same time as Palmer and with the addition of Nick Graham on vocals and bass, Atomic Rooster was born. Things hadn't been working out well for anyone in The Crazy World Of Arthur Brown. Palmer recalled that Brown had "gone missing on a commune on Long Island" and that was pretty much that. Atomic Rooster went through a number of personnel changes in a short period of time and their first album was released in 1970. Meanwhile, Palmer received a call from Keith Emerson to audition for a new group. He left Atomic Rooster in the summer of 1970.

Despite Palmer's early days in the premier league of rock music, his interest in classical music had always been there. "My grandfather was a professor of music at the Royal Academy, his brother was a classical percussionist, their mother — my great-great grandmother — was a classical guitar player, so I've always been interested in that sort of music," he said. "One of my first jazz albums was one of Jacques Loussier's *Play Bach* series. I always thought [playing classical material] was a great way to go."

****

So how did the iconic trio of Emerson, Lake and Palmer actually meet? Lake explained; "Keith and I met at the Fillmore West in San Francisco. At that very time I saw Keith, he was also thinking of moving, changing direction. Carl was playing with a group called Atomic Rooster, and we were friendly with Robert Stigwood, who was the manager of the group. We talked with Robert and he said, 'You know, I know this very, *very* good drummer, who you should look at'."

A lot of thought went into what to name the new group. The following names had been given some serious consideration: Triton, Triumvirate, and also, Seahorse. Eventually, the name of Emerson, Lake and Palmer was settled upon in order to remove the focus from Emerson as the most famous of the three. After all, the group didn't want to be thought of as the new Nice!

Based on his time with The Nice, Keith Emerson was voted as *Melody Maker*'s top pianist/organist. ELP was voted the International Brightest Hope. As Emerson said in hindsight, "not bad for a band that had never played a note on stage yet."

The accolade was an understandable one though. Even as a new band, each member of ELP already had a strong reputation behind them — both in terms of what they had done in the studio as well as live. Whilst Lake had the iconic and highly successful *In The Court Of The Crimson King* to his name, Emerson already had four albums — *The Thoughts of Emerlist Davjack* (1968), *Ars Longa Vita Brevis* (1968), *Nice* (1969) and *Five Bridges* (1970) — under his belt from his time with The Nice (with the latter two albums having reached number three and number two respectively in the UK). Equally, Arthur Brown was a household name by the time ELP were just getting going and although drummers themselves rarely become such, Carl Palmer's CV was enough to prove that he too was an excellent candidate for what was being billed by so many as the new supergroup.

In many ways, the pressure was on. Lake told *Beat Instrumental*; "If you could imagine the problems that faced this band when we started. We had to live down The Nice for a start, which wasn't easy since we had the main element of The Nice with us. Then, we only had a few weeks to get an act on the road and an album made. It had to be unpretentious and it had to set a direction for all of us at the same time. Incredibly difficult, as you can imagine. We purposely had to avoid doing press, but we knew that eyes were on us and we had to avoid giving people an excuse to accuse us of hype."

In *Melody Maker* in May 1970, Chris Welch reported on what was very early days for ELP; "Being witness to the birth of a band is always an exciting experience, and especially pleasing when the talents consist of three superb musicians like Keith Emerson, Greg Lake, and Carl Palmer. It was a privilege to hear the first tentative steps together of those who quit the security of three established bands — The Nice, King Crimson and Atomic Rooster — at a special preview at a London recording studio. The band had only played four times when I heard them at Island's half-built main studio in an old church in Notting Hill. Their representatives took pains to point out that they had only just started and were not entirely together. But the sounds that emerged were immediately startling and auger well for the future. Surprisingly, when one considers that they are already tipped as a major new force and have been under pressure to appear at this year's galaxy of festivals, the group have been having serious problems, the main one being a place to rehearse."

"There were several complaints about the noise as they thundered away — Carl 'The Basher' Palmer contributing one of his phenomenal drum solos, Greg buzzing his bass until the floor began to vibrate, and Keith tipping his organ around to obtain the frightening effects he made famous with The Nice. On bearding them in their lair, they were grappling with a piece of contemporary music by Béla Bartók, which sounded quite remarkable in their dextrous hands. They paused for deep conversation about the placing of accents, Keith peering across his grand piano to Carl concentrating furiously on drum patterns..."

"They treated me to a fast and furious version of 'Rondo' with Carl disappearing in a blur of hair and drumsticks as he attacked his snare, bass and tom-toms with brutal strength. 'And there's more where that came from', he gasped later. A version of '21st Century Schizoid Man' set my teeth on edge, aggravated by the vibration of the flooring, which in turn caused a stream of complaints from the studio below. They have to work a lot on material and arrangements. But the raw resources are there and when they are ready to explode upon us — BAZONKA! Hey, that's not a bad name for a group." (Emerson played the organ at Chris Welch's wedding on 4th December 1971).

Greg Lake reminisced in his (posthumously published) autobiography;

"From the very first few bars we played together, I could sense there was a very special chemistry between the three of us. We started with 'Rondo', which Keith had adapted from Dave Brubeck's jazz classic, 'Blue Rondo à la Turk', for The Nice's first album."

Following several rehearsal sessions at Island Studios in Notting Hill, ELP established their initial live set. It consisted of 'The Barbarian', 'Rondo', 'Nut Rocker' and *Pictures At An Exhibition*.

Stoked to get out there and play, Emerson said; "We are incredibly frustrated by not being able to get out and play to a live audience now. As soon as we do anything that pleases us, we want to let other people hear it. It's an incredible buzz to play live to a few people and an even bigger buzz to play before an audience as huge as the Isle of Wight will be."

The band's first live gig took place on 23rd August 1970 at the Plymouth Guildhall. A local band by the name of Earth was the support act. It was reported in *New Musical Express* in August 1970; "Emerson, Lake and Palmer made their world debut on Sunday at Plymouth Guildhall. The group strolled on stage looking somewhat nervous, somewhat apprehensive. They'd been rehearsing for four months and this was the test. 'This is what we sound like', said Keith Emerson, and the group launched into 'Barbarian', a thundering wall of sound with Keith playing two Hammond organs at the same time and Greg Lake pumping at his fuzz bass. The music had a feeling of power, of indestructible strength and the capacity audience were unleashed. Then 'Take A Pebble', a more fragile number with Keith plucking at the piano strings and then Greg switching to acoustic guitar, his voice floating out smoothly with Keith now on electric harpsichord. Next, a forty-minute composition, aptly titled *Pictures At An Exhibition*, a series of musical paintings and musical modes. *Pictures* saw the debut of the Moog synthesiser, weird electric sounds, sometimes harsh and angry and sometimes soft and soothing. Throughout, Carl Palmer bent over his drums, sometimes smiling at Greg who stood solid like a three-hundred-year-old oak tree. Emerson's showmanship was exceptional as he attacked his instruments in an orgy of visual excitement. Suddenly *Pictures* was over and the group were walking off stage, sweating and happy. The audience wanted more, much more. E. L. and P. returned and 'Rondo' — tighter and more forceful than ever before — blasted out. Then another encore. 'Remember this?' said Keith, as he led into 'Nut Rocker' once more. As Keith, Greg and Carl finally walked off, shirtless and exhausted, the audience stood on their chairs shouting, clapping, whistling, stamping their feet. For a full quarter-of-an hour the hopeful shouts of 'more, more' filled the concert hall. Emerson, Lake and Palmer had arrived."

Palmer said years later; "Our first show was at the Plymouth Guildhall,

From The Beginning

ahead of the Isle of Wight Festival of August 1970. It only held about 430 people, so it was a pretty small venue. But we went down a storm and earned around £400."

It was still relatively humble beginnings though; ELP travelled to the gig in a transit van that had previously been owned by Yes. The logic behind playing in a small venue outside of London was to ensure that if things didn't go well on the night, the embarrassment would be less public and ideally, minimised. Fortunately though, the gig went well, which was just as well considering the anticipation from the music press.

A journalist wrote for *Record Mirror* in 1970; "Emerson, Lake and Palmer are about to come amongst us following their debut at the Isle of Wight on August 30th and if they have managed to fuse those individual talents which contributed so much to The Nice, King Crimson and Atomic Rooster, we could well be blessed with the most exciting sound since the late lamented Cream."

Lake explained; "Having a good deal of experience in playing live shows with our previous bands, we had the good sense to insist on having our inaugural show somewhere a bit more out of the way and less conspicuous, so the very first show of ELP took place in front of eight-hundred people at the Guildhall in Plymouth on Sunday 23rd August 1970. We were nervous. I had barely performed in front of an audience since December 1969 and Carl and Keith had both been away from the stage for a few months too. And here we were, playing live together for the very first time as well as playing material no one had ever heard before — 'The Barbarian', 'Take A Pebble' and the full-length three-quarters-of-an-hour version of *Pictures At An Exhibition* as well as 'Rondo'. Keith kicked off the concert with the simple words, 'This is what we sound like'. We ended up getting a fifteen-minute standing ovation and I felt a deep sense of relief as I drove back home to London."

When ELP performed at the Isle of Wight Festival, Emerson had put in a memorable performance there with The Nice the previous year and in some ways, expectations were high. It was reported in the *Middlesex County Press* in September 1970; "Nearly half-a-million people from Britain, Europe and America braved the cold nights and lived in near-primitive conditions to listen to some of today's top musicians at the Isle of Wight Festival. A town of its own had been created where total freedom reigned. Pseudo-hippies who were frowned upon in suburbia found thousands and thousands like themselves. Now, the group of holidaymakers taking strolls through 'Freedom City' between their hotel meals felt out of place. Many people came unprepared for sleeping in the open. The St. John Ambulance dealt with hundreds of people suffering from exposure, and hot soup was dished out to shivering thousands. Sanitation was appalling. The only available lavatories consisted of trenches surrounded by corrugated fences. If you were one of the thousands who paid to go into the main arena and ended up a quarter-mile from the stage, then you probably wasted your money. The best view was free — from East Aston Down, nicknamed 'Devastation Hill'. Many French and Germans who believed that pop festivals should be free, camped here. Ironically they proved to be right, as a cool easterly wind was blowing throughout, taking sounds up the hill. Many people who had bought three-day tickets for £3 discovered this and tried to sell them at the entrance gate. The organisers, Fiery Creations, retaliated by telling people not to buy tickets at the main gate because a number of them had been forged. The island burst into sound on the Wednesday and thousands who had been camping outside moved into the arena for a free show lasting until early Friday morning. Except for Black Widow, all were little-known groups. Friday was the first fee-paying day with Chicago, Family, Taste and Procol Harum taking the limelight. On Saturday, Tiny Tim wooed the audience with his falsetto rendition of 'Tiptoe Through The Tulips' and 'There'll Always Be An England'."

"Performances from Emerson, Lake and Palmer went down well, as did John Sebastian, Ten Years After, The Doors, Sly and The Family Stone and, of course, The Who, whose wild rhythmic sound does not seem to have changed much since their unknown days, playing in Harrow about seven years ago. By Sunday, the festival grounds had become squalid. Waste abounded and water from the loos mixed with the mud to form a marshy expanse. The Jimi Hendrix Experience managed to get thousands out of their sleeping bags to dance in the night. It was an incredible sight. People, waving their arms in the air, were silhouetted against the smoke-filled sky. Then the soft, plaintive sounds of Joan Baez and Leonard Cohen — the last two acts — sent the ravers to sleep again. People listened to the music huddled together in sleeping bags. Others had rugs to keep them warm. Despite bad stage management, with gaps of sometimes half-an-hour between acts, the fans were appreciative. The artists were flops if their finale came without the shout of 'more, more!'. The beach at Freshwater Bay provided an occasional haven from the music. Here, hundreds of boys and girls stripped off to sun and sea bathe. Drug pushers in the crowd came straight out with 'want any acid, man?' while plain clothes detectives dressed like hippies pounded their beat through Freedom City. This tactic proved unpopular but effective. A collection for those who had been "busted" raised £16,000. Many stallholders ruthlessly exploited the crowd as demand exceeded supply. Peaches were a shilling each. Eleven-penny yoghurts went for 1s 6d and shilling cans of coke were sold for

From The Beginning

double the price. Despite objections, the festival was a success, and as one of the residents said: 'It's marvellous to see so many people enjoying themselves. It's proved the old colonels wrong who said the island would be wrecked'."

Whilst the report didn't put the spotlight on ELP, it really sets the scene in terms of what the Isle of Wight Festival perhaps felt like in 1970. The sensory elements of the festival are really brought to life by the way the journalist described the event, and it certainly shows the scale of the crowd that ELP performed to at a key appearance in their career. Lake told *Classic Rock* in October 2007; "The enduring memory is the actual physical sight of that many people. I suppose before that, the only time you'd see that many people gathered together would have been a war. The night before, we'd played to something like one-thousand people. The next day it was 600,000... There was a kind of random chaos taking place. In a way, it was all meant to be relaxed and 'peace, love, and have a nice day' but there was a kind of tension about the whole thing."

The scale of the festival was such that it still drew a lot of attention to ELP. Lake recalled; "After that festival, the very next day, ELP was on the front page of every music newspaper. It was indeed one of those overnight sensations." It was reported in *New Musical Express* in August 1970 under the headline of "Isle Of Wight Stars"; "Two of the saddest events in pop music during the past few months have been the breakup of The Nice and various members of King Crimson leaving to go their own ways. But out of that has come something brand new and very promising — Emerson, Lake and Palmer."

Lake explained; "We were extremely excited to have this incredible opportunity so early on in the band's career, but at the same time we were quite nervous about playing at such a big event before we even had a chance to get the show broken in and under control. In this sense, it really was a trial by fire."

Skilled showmen that they were, and not ones to miss an opportunity, Emerson and Lake set off cannons at the end of *Pictures At An Exhibition*. Prior to the performance, Emerson had tested the cannons in a field that was close to Heathrow Airport. Lake enthused on how at "the very end of our experimental arrangement of *Pictures At An Exhibition*, when Keith and I triggered the two cannons on stage, it was an unbelievable once-in-a-lifetime moment when the entire audience rose to their feet and gave the band a standing ovation."

Also: "We decided to fire these nineteenth-century cannons at the end of *Pictures At An Exhibition* — to emulate the *1812 Overture*. Unknown to us, the road crew had doubled the charge in the cannons. All I can remember was seeing this huge, solid-iron cannon leave the ground! It blew a couple of people off the stage. Luckily there was no cannonball in it. Thank God!"

The predominant narrative of ELP's history today seems to be that the Isle of Wight Festival was a dead-cert in putting the band on the road to success. At the time though, not every review was positive. As a result, there were a number of interviews in which the group were keen to assert what their creative intentions were, and indeed, how the negative press had affected them.

It was asserted in *Beat Instrumental* in January 1971; "To weld together a group of this stature, accomplishment and potential is extremely difficult. Greg Lake, although naturally hurt by some of the more waspish critics, is more sad than angry at their failure to perceive something fresh and new." To which Lake was quoted; "The pity is that now is the most beautiful time to catch anything, in its early days. The energy is vital and alive, and this is when people ought to be enthusiastic. It's like a flower just coming up through the earth. You go SMASH! Like that, it'll still live, it'll crawl around under the surface for a while, because it's got strength in the roots, and it'll come up again. But you've missed the beauty of the first push through."

It was reported in the same feature; "Almost immediately afterwards (post-Plymouth Guildhall gig), it was Isle of Wight time and, like many another artist, they received mixed receptions. Some raved, others scoffed. The more notorious pundits of the musical press inflated their outraged egos and let fly. Others, less rigid in their outlook, saw beyond the apathetic vibes of the "Festival" — but there is no doubt that ELP were wounded by the mainly negative press of their first international appearance."

Lake said of the Isle of Wight gig to *Melody Maker* in February 1971; "We put on a bad performance and we were setting ourselves up for judgement. That would have been okay if we had played well but we couldn't because the festival itself was so badly organised — the PA and everything — and we rely so much on the equipment being just right. The criticism there was just, but it was still poor. If they had written in the papers that the band played a bad set because the conditions were not right — but they didn't. After that we sort of got scrubbed out and nobody took any notice. The good part about the band was just left unnoticed and it is a source of pride to us that the (debut) LP sold an incredible amount of records, and we didn't push it or hype it in there. It was just bought by people who dug us on the tour… I had expected criticism, but it is still a hard pill to swallow. It gets through to you. But I think we have now gone through the stage where people are judging us. And really, I don't hold it

From The Beginning

against anybody who scratched us."

Prior to the Isle of Wight performance, other key venues and events had been discussed as potentials for ELP's major performance. So much so that in July 1970, *Melody Maker* reported; "Emerson, Lake and Palmer will not be appearing at the National Jazz, Blues and Pop Festival in Plumpton. Explained Keith Emerson: 'It appeared that if we did Plumpton, we'd be in a bill-topping position and we're not into that. We want to earn that position by the music we're playing, and not on the strength of the names of the groups we were in before.' They spent two days recording at Advision Studios last week. Recorded was the Greg Lake song 'Take A Pebble', an instrumental written by the group titled 'Barbarian', and a new version of 'Rondo'."

On the decision to play at the Isle of Wight Festival, Emerson had told a journalist prior to the performance; "We just thought it would be as well to play to as many people as possible, and being just one of the groups on the bill doesn't put us in the position of having to prove ourselves as headliners just yet. The only thing which does concern us is that there are obvious sound problems playing in the open air and as some of our things are acoustic or quite light and intricate, the sound can get to the edge of the stage and just crawl off."

ELP's first tour spanned from September 1970 to March 1971. It included dates in the UK and Europe.

It was reported in *Melody Maker* in October 1970; "Emerson, Lake and Palmer must be the brightest hopes for many a long year. Reputation alone won them their award in the *Melody Maker* poll and now they are proving themselves. At Watford last Thursday, they had a capacity crowd stamping and cheering as they pounded through material old and new with the ruthless competence and exaggerated showmanship that Keith Emerson inspires. Comparisons with The Nice are inevitable but here is a trio that takes off where The Nice stopped. With only three appearances behind them before the Watford gig, they could be forgiven for taking a while to warm up, but once they did there was no stopping them."

"Keith Emerson and Moog is a combination that had to happen. Having squeezed every possible sound from his Hammonds, the Moog was the natural progression — and the £4,000 computer-like gadget that sits amid the speakers brings out a variety of space-fiction noises once reserved for the studio only. Greg Lake and Carl Palmer assure you it's not a mark two version of The Nice. Greg uses acoustic guitar on several numbers, playing almost classical style, and takes the vocal seat, while Carl's drumming holds the whole thing together. Speed is his greatest asset as he proved in his solo during 'Rondo'."

"'Rondo' is the only Nice number ELP feature and the arrangement has been changed to suit the new trio. But it still brings out the most in Keith, dressed in glittery tail suit, who leaps on to his organ and chucks his knife into the speaker cabinet. *Pictures At An Exhibition* — Keith's major new opus — showed us what the Moog is capable of, though Keith admits he is still learning how to use it. Dramatic vocals, a wah-wah bass solo, some slick replying between bass and drums and organ and tasteful acoustic guitar work, make up this twenty-minute piece, which brought the fans to their feet. 'Take A Pebble', Greg Lake's composition, features Keith plucking the piano strings inside the lid and perfect brush work from Carl, and 'Knife-Edge' shows the band at its heaviest. For an encore they gave us a rockin' version of the old B. Bumble number, 'Nut Rocker', which had the idiot dancers bopping in the aisles. An ideal climax to a show which proved that ELP are worthy of their brightest hope award."

2.
From The Flight Of The Seagull

Emerson, Lake and Palmer's debut studio album was of an eponymous title. It was released in the UK in November 1970 on Island Records. The album's initial North American release was several weeks later, in January 1971, on Atlantic Records' Cotillion Records subsidiary. It went to number four in the UK and on the Billboard 200 in the US, it got to number eighteen. It got to number seventeen in Canada on three separate occasions, the first of which was 8th May — it stayed in the top one-hundred for thirty-five weeks.

Recording of the album began in July 1970 at Advision Studios when ELP were still yet to perform live. A journalist writing for *Record Mirror* in 1970 was lucky enough to speak to Emerson whilst it was still being worked on. They described what they witnessed upon their visit to the BBC rehearsal rooms: "I heard two of the tracks which the group have completed for that album — a twelve-minute opus titled 'Take A Pebble' and four minutes of hard exciting rock on 'The Barbarian', on which Carl Palmer contributes his exciting rhythmic patterns and Greg Lake adds a new dimension to Emerson's keyboard virtuosity, with his scraped soul vocals."

Emerson told the journalist; "Both Greg and Carl have something entirely different to offer from me and that in itself has given us new directions. We are learning from each other. On our next album we are allotting three separate tracks to each individual so that it is fair shares for all. We hope to avoid the mistakes made by groups like Blind Faith by working out individual policies and seeing that each member has a say in what is going on. There are no leaders in this group."

Released as a single in 1970, 'Lucky Man' charted in the US and in Canada. It got to number forty-eight on the Billboard Hot 100. It also got into the top twenty in the Netherlands. It was re-released in 1973 and charted again in the US and Canada. In 1971, *Billboard* described the song as being "loaded with programming appeal and should make its mark on the sales charts". When Lake presented the song to Emerson and Palmer, the three of them improvised arrangements for it. ELP's treatment of the song showcases one of rock music's earliest uses of a Moog synthesiser solo.

Even when ELP's debut album was still in the works, upon being asked if the band had a singles policy, Emerson explained; "If something happens which obviously fulfils the function and requirements of a hit single, we will release it. It's not something we have talked about. It is something that will either happen naturally or not at all." It just goes to show what 'Lucky Man' was worth.

For years to come, Lake would go on to explain the origins of 'Lucky Man' across a number of interviews. When his mother gave him his first guitar, the first chords he picked up were D, A minor, E minor, and G. He wrote 'Lucky Man' within the scope of his early knowledge of those chords. It came to be used on ELP's debut album when the group were in need of one more song. When Lake first played the song to Emerson and Palmer, they were initially unimpressed. They were also unsure of whether the feel of it would be a good fit for the album overall. Lake then worked on the song in the studio with Palmer. He added multiple overdubs of bass, triple-tracked acoustic guitars, electric guitar, and harmony vocals until it sounded convincing. This particular recording of the song is featured on the deluxe edition of the debut album. It also has a second electric guitar solo in place of where Emerson would later come in to overdub his Moog solo. Emerson's Moog synthesiser solo was recorded in one take. The solo begins as a low drone on D before it shoots up by two octaves and glides distinctively throughout.

'Lucky Man' stands out as a unique component of ELP's eponymous album; unlike many of the songs that richly made use of a distorted fuzz bass, 'Lucky Man' is of a more acoustic nature overall. The lyrics tell the story of a man who had everything but died when he went to war.

Lake considered of the song; "I truly cannot remember everything about writing it, other than I think it struck me as being a sort of minstrel type of event with these chords, G, D, E minor and A minor. 'Lucky Man' has kind of an almost medieval element tone to it. It is like a medieval folk song in a way. That was the essence of the idea. I wrote the song in its entirety and I finished it and I remembered it… You cannot disassociate the tune, the song has been very lucky for me. It came about because of a piece of good fortune, which was my mother giving me the guitar and it has been lucky for me ever since. I would say if I was going to be honest, I have been very lucky in life."

ELP's first album and indeed 'Lucky Man' were, in some ways, unlikely successes. The latter is just over four-and-a-half-minutes long — this would have made it something of a risk in terms of getting radio play. Also, the track showcases an unusual range of instrumentation in that it contains a Moog solo. Not only that, but a Moog solo that makes liberal use of portamento (pitch sliding from one note to another). 'Lucky Man' is a very unique-sounding track and it is plausible that the odds may have been against it commercially. Nevertheless though, the single helped to sell the album.

The Moog is a distinctive feature throughout the whole album, and certainly, a trademark of ELP's sound. Lake confirmed of the track, 'Take A Pebble', when responding to a reader's question in *Melody Maker* in October 1971; "The pebble sound was achieved on the Moog synthesiser. We used reverb on it to get a sound like water dripping in a cave."

Emerson said of the *Emerson, Lake and Palmer* album in 1974; "Atlantic records decided to release 'Lucky Man' in America. We were in England at the time before we knew about it. I wasn't too pleased about it, but the way it goes, the records are usually handed out to the DJs and they play the ones they like and they use the shortest ones. It's quite a commercial song to an extent and it's possibly from that point of view that it was used. It's quite easy to relate to. It was never released in England. I didn't have any pre-conceived ideas about it (the first ELP album) doing that well. Something like 'Knife-Edge' would have been a bit more representative at the time."

"That was right at the beginning, we had no choice. I hadn't even met the people from Atlantic, because we were still in England. It was only after I got to America that I realised that it had been out and that it had done this and it had done that. Atlantic were pleased because it was selling the album. A lot of people liked it, they were obviously buying it. It was really the people's choice. It is a shame that we really can't perform it the same way it is on the album. There's a lot of double-tracked vocals. Greg's playing electric, bass and acoustic guitar on it. If we had really thought about it, and we ourselves, had wanted to release it as a single, then we would have considered these points, and possibly re-arranged it so we could have done it some way on stage. Now we come out and people want to hear it. Greg performs it as an acoustic piece and I guess it's rather disappointing to some people because they want to hear the recorded version. There we were, in the position of it having been released and us not knowing that people want to hear it, and the way it was done on the album being impossible for us to do on stage. It's a throw-in thing."

On the first album, it is evident that Emerson was influenced by Béla Bartók. He said as much himself in a number of interviews and the percussive use of piano on the album very much showcases this.

Upon being asked whether ELP's first album was a statement of intent, Carl Palmer said in later years; "I don't think the first album really said that's how we are. Keith Emerson wanted to play three organ pieces, which had no relation to the group at all, really. It didn't involve the other members, and I thought that was rather strange. There was a song thrown in at the end called 'Lucky Man', because we were short on time, and that turned out to be a big hit. Keith and I wrote 'Tank', which was a nice coming-together. It was a bit of a hodgepodge, but because it was so quintessentially English, and because it was so different, it did catch on. There was one very strong rock track, 'Knife-Edge'. It all came together very quickly. I think that it was recorded in two weeks."

Greg Lake explained; "When ELP was formed, such was the buzz around the band that expectations were very quickly flying high and within days we were being asked for a date when we thought we could deliver the first album."

The eponymous debut album was reviewed in the *Reading Evening Post* in December 1970; "The last twelve months have seen fantastic exchanges in the world of so-called popular musicianship and composition has improved almost out of recognition, and the divisions of classic, jazz and pop under which the less enlightened record departments love to list their wares has narrowed to be almost ridiculous. Never were these facts better illustrated than on this absolutely superb album. Although the three titles on side one are sufficient evidence of the trio's outstanding talent, it is 'The Three Fates' suite on the reverse that really takes one's breath away. After only a single hearing I'd rank it among my top three records of the year."

It was advocated in the *Coventry Evening Telegraph* in December 1970; "Emerson, Lake and Palmer are choice among the progressive groups on the college circuit. Their self-titled LP on Island shows why. The music is sufficiently unusual to be distinctive, yet it has enough to be consistently appealing."

It was considered in the *Newcastle Journal* in December 1970; "Keith Emerson, organist with The Nice, is moving on to still greater things with the help of guitarist Greg Lake (ex-King Crimson) and Carl Palmer (ex-Atomic Rooster). The trio's first Island album is already high in the charts, as it richly deserves to be. The three-part suite that opens the second side of the LP is an imaginative exercise in fusing classical music and jazz-pop, with Emerson on top form on the Royal Festival Hall organ. When he masters his Moog synthesiser, there should be no stopping them."

From *Beat Instrumental* in January 1971: "Emerson's classical influences are still there, of course. It takes more than a few months to subdue such a dominant musical trait. Nevertheless, it is easy to hear that the more melodic character of Lake's music is already making itself felt. On the *Emerson, Lake and Palmer* album (which has confounded the earlier pundits by proving and infuriatingly massive seller) there is a composition called 'Take A Pebble', in which Greg shows himself the originator of the softer side of ELP. Written and sung by Lake, 'Take A Pebble' opens with brushed chords on piano strings, leading into gentle bass and lyrics from Greg. These, in turn, evolve into an expounded development on piano from Keith, finally returning to a re-statement of the opening theme. Keith's piano-playing is just one of the many surprises on this album. It seems to be his natural instrument — even more than the organ — and he makes use of some highly original and creative work, sounding almost Gershwin-esque at times in his efforts to combine classicism, romanticism and twentieth-century modes. On organ, however, Emerson returns to his best-known forte, and 'Knife-Edge', the heaviest number on the LP, gives him chance to catch the pulse of the listener with his unique and demoniac style. 'Knife-Edge' is, in some ways, the most representative ELP sound (as it appears in this album). Brooding, fierce and frightening, it is a vocal showcase for Lake, as well as a complete vehicle for the more percussive talents of both Carl Palmer and Keith Emerson."

The album was reviewed in the *Buckinghamshire Examiner* in December 1970; "Emerson, Lake and Palmer are names that have been bandied around pop critic circles for a long time. Everyone has been expecting so much from their debut album. And now it is on sale, there is a wave of criticism directed at the band. This is probably a good thing because the band are so good and total acceptance from the start might well stunt their growth. Now they can study themselves in the harsh and painful glare of adverse opinion. Carl's drumming is so different from his work with Atomic Rooster. His power and technique have been channelled, and he is so much looser and more inventive. Keith Emerson seems to be getting more into contemporary classics and is vaguely similar to Stan Kenton. He is one of a few who come anywhere near exploring the full possibilities of the Moog. The first side has three songs — 'The Barbarian', 'Take A Pebble' and 'Knife-Edge'. Here we have the chance of hearing Greg's folksy voice and acoustic guitar. Side two opens with church organ on 'The Three Fates', Keith doing his *Phantom Of The Opera* bit, dissolving into more beautiful piano. Emerson, Lake and Palmer have so much to say and offer. It would be a tragedy if they were stifled or discouraged by the knockers. They could become moodies."

This review really highlights the fact that upon the release of their debut album, ELP were in a very tentative position; whilst the album largely received positive critical acclaim and commercial success, it was still very early days.

Although ELP were being heralded as a new supergroup, from the record company's perspective, it still didn't make sense for them to expect the record-buying public to invest too heavily in the group. "We were going to release a double album to begin with," Emerson said at the time. "But the record company dissuaded us as it might be a too-expensive item to expect the public to buy from a new group."

It's fascinating to consider all of the possibilities that were still on the table during the early days of the band's tenure. In 1970, Emerson was asked if it was still a possibility that Robert Fripp would be joining ELP for some of their tour dates. His response: "It's most unlikely now, especially as we would have to get together with Bob to work out our new numbers and there is so little time for each of us. It certainly could not happen this year."

Despite cynicism from some critics, in terms of performances, things were going well overall. *New Musical Express* asserted in November 1970; "Criticism has been levelled against ELP, based in the main on Emmo's occasional use of Nice techniques and even the "unthinkable" use in the trios act of 'Rondo', very much a "Nice" possession. At the Isle of Wight this year, I was disappointed with what ELP did. Maybe this had something to do with the showmanship of the use of cannons and the calls from the crowd for familiar Nice numbers. Had we been expecting a re-birth of The Nice? More recently at the group's Royal Festival Hall concert, my opinion shifted by a good many degrees and I was able to appreciate the musical direction and undoubted combined talent of the three members. Although the packed crowd responded fanatically to the music, certain critics took it upon themselves to knock."

And indeed, Emerson was keen to address the fact that although many critics may have opted to focus on him — due to the fame he had acquired from being with The Nice — he was certain that it would just be a matter of time before ELP would be appreciated as a whole. "Everything we play, we mean. And we're not afraid of the criticism we receive," he said. "At the Festival Hall, a few critics decided to centre their attention on one area of the band — unfortunately they got only one third of the total sound effect. With the arrival of the album, the talents of Greg and

From The Flight Of The Seagull

Carl will become more apparent and they will get the recognition they deserve. ELP is both three individuals and a group and though it will be some time before the band is recognised as the latter, ELP has all the time in the world."

A different journalist had written for *New Musical Express* the previous week; "It must have been around 10:30pm on Monday night at the Royal Festival Hall, when Keith Emerson proved beyond all fear of contradiction that he is the supreme showman. While perched most precariously atop one of his brace of rather battered Hammond organs, roses cascaded around him, thunder flashes exploded and a magenta flare lit up the auditorium. Though the instrument line-up remains the same, it would be grossly unfair to the still-fresh memory of The Nice to compare ELP with their illustrious predecessor. They are two entirely different groups, with Emmo even more into producing basic sounds and enacting the part of the master's apprentice with his electronic Moog."

"Commencing with the extended work, *Pictures At An Exhibition*, Keith was soon to be seen leaping about the vast stage as he switched from organ-to-piano-to-Moog and back again with an almost casual abandon. In support, both Carl Palmer and Greg Lake and variations to the theme. During an interlude, Greg took up his acoustic guitar and sang in clear tones against a quite musical backdrop, prior to the threesome exploding into a crescendo of sight and sound. Which had a tinsel-clad Emerson playing games with a roving Moog keyboard."

"After an intermission which enabled the capacity audience to catch its breath, ELP reappeared and roared into an original composition called 'The Barbarian'. 'Take A Pebble' had Mr Emerson playing the strings of the piano as part of the introduction as Greg again featured himself as both singer and guitarist. Again, this number progressed into a frantic workout for everyone concerned. A much shorter composition, 'Knife-Edge', had the entire audience clapping their hands and supplying the basic beat to riff. The next selection, 'Rondo', re-kindled fond memories of past affiliations and proved to be a showcase for the drumnastics of Carl Palmer. For a finale it was a chuck of uninhibited rock in the form of 'Nut Rocker', and a cue for the massed idiot dancers to perform their freaked-out ballet. The response was ear-shattering."

Due to how Emerson, Lake and Palmer already had a wealth of individual commercial achievements behind them by the time they grouped together, it helped to promote their debut album.

"Emerson, Lake and Palmer, who have signed with Island Records and have their first LP out in November (featuring such items as 'The Barbarian' and 'Take A Pebble') are, of course, Keith Emerson, Greg Lake and Carl Palmer who appear at the City Hall on Sunday (October 4th)," reported the *Newcastle Evening Chronicle* in October 1970. "No self-respecting pop fan should need to be reminded that Keith (ex-Gary Farr and The T-Bones, and V.I.P.'s) really made a name for himself with The Nice, or that he was voted top international keyboard player in *Melody Maker*'s widely respected poll. Greg Lake was with King Crimson, who became the talking point of the Rolling Stones' free Hyde Park concert last year, and Carl Palmer joined Emerson and Lake via Chris Farlowe and The Thunderbirds, The Crazy World Of Arthur Brown and an outfit called Atomic Rooster. The three make a formidable combination and Emerson, Lake and Palmer strike me as being well able to live up to having been voted the most promising new group in the aforementioned poll."

Everyone in ELP brought a high level of skill and professionalism to the table. Not only that, but there was probably also a sense that collectively, all three musicians inspired each other to keep getting better and better.

3.
People Are Stirred

The extent of pressure on ELP and their anxiety about the press was an ongoing theme at times. Lake told *Disc & Music Echo* in 1971; "We must be the hardest-working band. I've never had this amount of pressure before. It's good because we're successful. But it's bad because our nerves suffer. One minute you open a paper and see your album's number one, the next your hands are shaking. It's that sort of pressure."

Keen to strike while the iron was hot (but also in debt and in need of an album to recoup costs and become a profitable band), ELP began to work on their second studio album in January 1971. Following their 1970 European tour, the band returned to Advision Studios in London, to begin work on new material. From playing together on the tour, Emerson was mindful of how he and Palmer had been exploring more complex rhythmic ideas. Referring to some patterns that Palmer had been playing on practice drum pads, the keyboard player found that they complemented some of the runs that he had been playing on the piano. This informed the basis for the music on *Tarkus*. The group's approach to the album was to have 'Tarkus' as the conceptual centrepiece for the album even before a firm story — or even theme — had been considered.

Of course, further down the line, the band established this, and firmly so. As Lake explained, the song is about "the futility of conflict, expressed in this context in terms of soldiers and war — but it's broader than that. The words are about revolution, the revolution that's gone, that has happened. Where has it got anybody? Nowhere". He went on to describe the track, which opens with the 'Eruption' section — an instrumental in 5/4 time — as having a "frustrating" meter. He added that the lyrical songs that follow, concern "the hypocrisy of it all", referring to the closing march at the end as "a joke". (With 'Tarkus' being just under twenty-one minutes long, ELP would not record a longer piece in the studio until 1973, with 'Karn Evil 9' being just shy of half-an-hour in length.)

Emerson said; "The imagery of the armadillo kept hitting me. It had to have a name. Something guttural. It had to begin with the letter 'T' and end with a flourish. *Tarka The Otter* may have come into it, but this armadillo needed a science fiction kind of name that represented Charles Darwin's theory of evolution in reverse. Some mutilation of the species caused by radiation... 'Tarkus'!"

As a suite in seven parts, 'Tarkus' is one of the earliest multipart progressive rock songs. The odd numbered sections are instrumentals, and the even numbered ones include vocals. It is a concept piece whereby not only is the overall idea embedded in the music and lyrics alone, but also from the album artwork and the section titles. That said, to the listener, the concept and narrative is ambiguous and is certainly open to interpretation.

The short songs on side two are unrelated to 'Tarkus' and indeed, each other. 'The Only Way (Hymn)' includes themes from Bach's Toccata and Fugue in F major (BWV 540) and Prelude and Fugue VI (BWV 851). Although not credited, 'Are You Ready Eddy?' was predominately inspired by Bobby Troup's 1956 song, 'The Girl Can't Help It'. Emerson referred to the track as "an impromptu jam" played in celebration of completing work on *Tarkus*.

Notably, when the band were working on *Tarkus*, side two was plausibly something of an afterthought compared to the material on side one. Lake told *Melody Maker* in February 1971; "We have no clue, none whatsoever, of the second side. We are due in the studio on Tuesday and we have nothing at all."

The making of *Tarkus* wasn't all plain sailing. Lake was frustrated that Emerson chose to play in keys that were not a good fit for his voice. Also, Lake wasn't happy with the album's title track. After a band meeting with management, he was persuaded to record the song but as a compromise, he contributed his original composition, 'Battlefield'. Such were the tensions of the 'Tarkus' suite that Lake nearly left the band over the whole thing. He eventually got on board with the project but evidently, even at a relatively early stage in their tenure, it is clear that ELP consisted of strong-minded individuals.

In The Nice, Emerson had been used to being the leader. Although bassist Lee Jackson and drummer Brian Davison had voiced their views, Emerson had always had the final word. Equally, having worked with Robert Fripp in King Crimson, Lake was no stranger to having to hold his own within the dynamics of a strong-minded band.

"ELP never argued over money, never argued over any women, never argued over any affairs like that. The only thing we'd argue over would be music. We could argue over four bars for about four years," said Palmer with hindsight. "Yes, there were some real tensions within ELP, but that's good, to tell you the truth. You always get someone who wants to play a little bit safe and you always get somebody who wants to turn it up. Because I wasn't one of the main writers, my position was as a referee between those two. I wouldn't side with anyone — I would say exactly what I thought about the music, about what they played or sung."

He added; "They would take it from me if I said that something was not that good or that I didn't like the writing. I mean, no one else would ever go up to them, no one from the record company, the management, it wouldn't happen that way. There was an inner trust, which ran very deep. They knew I wasn't going to walk in with a carrier bag of songs and say, 'This is what we should be playing'. I was about trying to get the best out of everyone and they understood that. Greg trusted me implicitly on that score. There were moments between us, of course, there are always going to be moments, but I'll tell you what, not one of us ever sat on the fence. We each had a role and although I wasn't a writer, my position was about the organisation of the band, which I got involved with in a big way. I'd write everything down and make sure everybody was literally on the same page. We all had a part to play; we wanted Greg to write us the three-minute songs that'd get us on the radio and Keith to steer the boat toward the prog rock that we all wanted."

Tensions aside, everyone got their heads together. *Tarkus* was a strong album commercially and musically and it didn't take too long to record either. Emerson said, "*Tarkus* was like a testing ground for us, I think, mainly because of the time changes and key changes. I think it was a good start for us to get into doing something that was really experimental. To that extent, it means a lot to me." Lake said, "It took six days to record *Tarkus*. I don't know whether that's because there are so few people in the band, but I'm sure that doing an album quickly helps to make it sound fresh. If you spend four days on one song you lose a lot, whereas you can maintain one-hundred-percent energy if you only do it for a day. There is a danger in becoming analytical. In some ways you score, but in others you dip badly. If you take out a note because it's slightly flat, you lose the rawness and aggression."

The contrast between the two sides of the *Tarkus* LP served as an excellent vehicle to showcase not only each band member's ability as individuals, but as a team. Lake told *Melody Maker* in 1971; "The first album was a balance, but it was a balance of individuals. There was Keith and I — but this time it (*Tarkus*) is together. He has written for me and I have written for him. Breaking it down to basics, I suppose you could say that the instrumental parts are Keith's and the songs are mine. The aim is to achieve a working balance where the output of each person is allowed freedom, yet the total gels as one music. In many bands, it happens that one person is musically not satisfied. What we've achieved is very pleasing, very pleasing indeed."

As ELP's second album, *Tarkus* was released in June 1971 on Island Records. It got to number one in the UK and to number nine in the US. It got to number twelve in Canada on two occasions that totalled four weeks.

Tarkus was reviewed in *Rolling Stone* (and generally, negatively so — it just goes to show that, at the time, nothing was to be taken for granted in terms of ELP's achievements): "Emerson, Lake and Palmer are very competent musicians, as rock performers go. They're agile, flamboyant, and sensitive to their instruments' limitations. You could easily go through *Tarkus* and, passage by passage, point out who they competently sound like: Zappa here, Black Sabbath there, Brian Auger, Dave Mason, Pink Floyd, Spirit. But in the end, all that's happened is that you've been competently reminded of lots of other performers and have been left with nothing unique by which to remember Emerson, Lake and Palmer."

"The Beatles turned their eclecticism to their advantage by stamping everything they synthesised with their own unmistakable insignia. Emerson, Lake and Palmer, musicians but not auteurs, have no personal mould in which to cast their music. Realising this deficiency, they've tried to compensate for it on their second album by arranging some of their material into a musical suite, a sort of tone poem for rock instrumentation: out of an erupting volcano, the giant beast *Tarkus* is born. Part armadillo, part Sherman tank, and part geodesic dome, Tarkus sets off across the land, destroying whatever monsters cross his path. After a showdown with the deadly Manticore (in which Tarkus loses an eye) our victorious anti-hero goes off into the deep sea. So what? you ask. Musically, the unfolding of this drama is as uninvolving as the sketch I've just given. Beneath the surface level all the dramatic conflict we're supposed to witness in the 'Tarkus' suite is non-existent. The melodic themes are incapable of capturing our allegiance, and the piece itself has no palpable purpose or justification for itself. Here's just one more example of a sound and fury, signifying nothing."

"The second side is less ambitious but much better than the first, in that Emerson, Lake and Palmer don't try to live beyond their means. Keith Emerson really shines on this side as the pop keyboard virtuoso that he is. 'Jeremy Bender', a fresh and bright song in the 'John Barleycorn' style, doesn't last a moment longer than it needs to. 'Bitches Crystal' and 'A Time And A Place' are the kind of numbers upon which Emerson, Lake and Palmer have built their concert reputation: fast, shiny, seemingly complex, but in essence glib and hollow stuff. Easily forgettable. 'The Only Way' is a pitiful composition infested to the core with fakey and fashionable religion. All this is preceded by a Bach Prelude, which was an incredibly bad choice on Emerson's part, since it only serves to show, by comparison, how shallow is their depth of religious feeling. Bach's music, expressive of the most committed religious states of mind, can be exalted or anguished; Emerson, Lake and Palmer's can be neither."

"'Infinite Space', the track on the album most worth paying attention to, has a nicely constructed system of rhythms. Emerson's left hand and Lake's bass take turns establishing an exotic foundation rhythm, while Emerson probes and spaces with his right. It's a muscular piece of music which, like Brubeck's '40 Days', reveals some of the lyric possibilities of a percussive piano style. And to match Emerson's Brubeck technique, Lake and Palmer on this cut sound like Brubeck's rhythm men Wright and Morello. 'Are You Ready Eddy?' is a good-humoured Little Richard-type bop. Emerson's playing is at its unselfconscious best, Lake's vocal has that John Lennon echo that we're all so accustomed to, and at the tail end of the number, there's a wonderfully inhuman whining that sounds as if it were coming straight from Yoko Ono's lips."

"*Tarkus* records the failure of three performers to become creators. Regardless of how fast and how many styles they can play. Emerson, Lake and Palmer will continue turning out mediocrity like *Tarkus* until they discover what, if anything, it is that they must say on their own and for themselves."

The album was reviewed in the *Thanet Times*; "The new single releases are looking totally uninspiring this week, so this space will be dedicated to reviewing the month's best albums. And with Emerson, Lake and Palmer topping the bill, who needs singles? The inimitable ELP's second album is now in the shops and many of their fans are likely to want a taste of their smooth harmonies and Moog synthesiser. Yes, *Tarkus* — that monster from the unknown so beloved to Keith, Carl and Greg — is bound to be a monster success. The activities of Tarkus take up the whole of side one and is a feature of their live dates. Back in April, Thanet ELP followers were treated to the creature's fiery escapades at Margate's Winter Gardens. And if the one-thousand-plus audience's response to the group's performance is anything to go by, this album will soon be in the possession of every one of those fans. The imagination runs riot as this side spins, the intermittent squeals of the Moog adding to the incredible atmosphere conjured up. Then it's back to reality on side two, where some good old rock 'n' roll in the form of 'Are You Ready Eddy?' brings us back to our senses. This track is a tribute to Eddy Offord, their engineer. On to more lighter sounds and it's 'Jeremy Bender', during which Keith excels on piano."

And in *The Record Songbook*: "Anything progressive is thought-provoking, even controversial, and Emerson, Lake and Palmer's second album — *Tarkus* on Island ILPS 9155 — has created a wide diversity of opinion among critics and reviewers. But devotees will come down on the side of greatness and rate *Tarkus* a natural progression from ELP's debut LP. If you listen to both albums this is made clear. The whole of side one is called 'Tarkus' and is one continuous track with themes running through it. One "movement" merges easily into the next, and the pattern is established with Lake's songs joined by Emerson's central theme. If you look at the inside sleeve pictures of the tank-like armadillo, you'll be able to see that the story is being followed in the music on the record. 'Battlefield' is the climax on side one and the theme seems to mingle with the song. Anti-war! Slow, dramatic, atmospheric and beautiful in parts. Brilliant ELP! 'Aquatarkus' ends the story with the armadillo walking out to sea. Emerson ends the side instrumentally as it began. Climatic and dramatic with the early theme apparent, ending with heavy discords and one final long chord. See this side as a complete suite, and you discover the excitement ELP intended. Side two is a set of different songs that have no connection at all with side one. 'The Only Way (Hymn)' on track three is the only classical Emerson on the record. He plays St Mark's Church organ and there is a very good song from Lake based on Toccata in F and Prelude VI (Bach). Notable piano and bass work on this. 'A Time And A Place' is incredible! Great Lake vocal on this fast raver, with good Hammond organ riff from Emerson. Palmer's drumming strong and to the point. Keith Emerson, Greg Lake and Carl Palmer have, in *Tarkus*, once again proved their undoubted superiority!"

Of 'Eruption', Justin Hayward of The Moody Blues wrote for *Melody Maker* in July 1971; "That sounds as if it was recorded backwards... It's great, busy, busy music. It's exciting and there's some great effects... I haven't heard it before, but I should have done. They are a great band. I really like Greg Lake. He is a great bass player."

Not long after the recording of *Tarkus*, ELP were on a roll with their live performances. It was reported in *Sounds* in April 1971; "ELP always have something new to offer on their gigs and Wednesday night at Leicester's De Montfort Hall was no exception. Not only did they play many of the established favourites but included two samples from the new album due out in May. 'Tarkus' — the title track taking up one side of the album — is a half-hour affair which shows all three musicians at their best. Starting in 5/4 time, the number progresses through innumerable time changes bringing it all up to the pitch of hysteria. There are some beautiful organ passages included, with the heated drumming of Carl powering the number on, and featuring poignant vocals of Greg, to the setting of his thoughtful and exact lead work. The second sampler — 'Jeremy Bender' — was a quick country tune with a jolly beat and a constant melody. And judging from the reception the numbers were given, the album is going to be a seller."

"In spite of a subdued start to the evening, ELP received standing ovations to most of the numbers from the 2,500 who filled the hall. *Pictures At An Exhibition* — with Keith playing the organ — opened the second set and they followed with 'Take A Pebble'. Keith now incorporates a lot more showmanship and comedy into the act — springing into the audience and creating some way-out sound effects. By the time the synthesised hissing of steam and chugging engines filled the hall, everybody was on their chairs ready for the inevitable 'Rondo'. The way Keith spans the organ, hurls it across the stage, and lies under it squeezing out grunts of electronic pain, makes me think he is trying to kill the last bit of The Nice left in him — which the music certainly does. The only possible encore was 'Nut Rocker', which brought the fans to the front of the stage, rocking with the band as they finished a night which bettered the gig there last year."

It was reported in *Melody Maker* in April 1971; "Emerson, Lake and Palmer performed the first pop concert in Wigan, a town generally deprived of progressive music, for over three years at the town's ABC cinema. The trio blew into the mill town like a TNT explosion last Thursday and played to an ecstatic audience of two-thousand and a handful of police officers. The tremendous reputation that has grown up around these three young musicians in such a short time was more than justified as Emerson and Co. displayed dexterity and total mastery over their instruments. They played jazz, rhythm and blues, classical and folk music with such subtle transitions that any anomalies between the styles went unnoticed before even the most competent progressive musician. The group revolved around Keith Emerson. As a showman he was terrific — dragging several hundredweights of Hammond organ across the stage that has regrettably become almost an anachronism in Wigan. Jumping over it and pulling it down onto the stage floor with him, Keith was playing two organs simultaneously for much of the night. He played the grand piano as if it were a guitar, coming down into the audience with a wailing portmanteau and disappearing into the Gents with it."

"Greg Lake and Carl Palmer were not without their moments. Lake's haunting, poignant voice and guitar solos came as peaceful contrasts to the World War Three sounds that thundered across the auditorium when the group was in full swing. Carl Palmer as the percussionist had the difficult job of keeping time for an ensemble that seems to play at twice the speed of the average group. An immaculate solo in the finale brought a fitting climax to his performance and three girls in the upstairs auditorium standing on their seats to display identical red-hot pants with the words 'Carl The Greatest'. The group played numbers from their first album, the title track of their forthcoming album, *Tarkus*, and as an item of nostalgia for fans of the now defunct Nice group, 'Rondo'."

Lake recalled; "The last show on this leg of the UK tour was played in Wigan on 1st April 1971. Not so many well-known bands came to play in Wigan so none of us really knew what to expect. As is often the case in smaller towns and cities though, the audience was fantastic. It was one of those special nights when everything just seemed to go right and the atmosphere in the room was truly electrifying. People often ask me to name my favourite ELP performance and, of course, the ones that often spring to mind are the big festivals and the more historic events. Looking back now however, I think that some of ELP's greatest performances took place in the small city halls in the United Kingdom and the United States during the early days of the band's career."

In the early seventies, many British musicians were welcomed by the US. When ELP were due to perform their 30th April/1st May dates at the Fillmore East in 1971, listed on the marquee canopy with them was John Mayall, Ten Years After, Procol Harum and Jethro Tull. The following review advocated highly of ELP's performance at the venue but it is starkly noticeable how the journalist writing for the local newspaper was keen to draw comparison between the band in question and The Nice. Still though, the review is a worthwhile one in terms of ELP because it is demonstrative of how, at barely a year into their tenure, their identity in their own right had yet to be solidified in the consciousness of some. Nevertheless, the journalist was complementary of Lake and Palmer's contribution:

"Leaving Fillmore East after seeing Emerson, Lake and Palmer, most of the members of the audience had one question on their minds, if not on their lips: did I just see a performance by a genius or a madman? Ever since the days of The Nice, Keith Emerson has been an energetic and unusual performer. On records, the three members of The Nice were all equal. But as the leader of the band and the man who played the featured instrument, Emerson did, naturally enough, stand out. On the whole, however, you were hearing a group, not a solo performer with a two-man back-up group. On stage, it was a totally different story. Emerson stood in the featured position on the stage and usually had more space for himself and his equipment than the other two members of the group combined.

People Are Stirred

At a Nice concert, Emerson had about two-thirds of the stage. He usually went on with a full Hammond organ, a small electrical organ, and a piano. In the course of the show, he used all three, and before the show was over, the smaller organ was usually in pieces all over the stage. As well as being an unbelievably good musician, Emerson also has a better-than-average knowledge of electronics. He used that knowledge to create weird sound effects, which can be heard on all of the live cuts by The Nice."

"On stage, Keith Emerson was The Nice. He dominated the show to the point where the other two members could have been replaced by a pair of unknowns at the last minute and no one would have known the difference. He has a sense of theatrics that surpasses most in the business. One of his favourite tricks during the days of The Nice was to actually play the organ with a pair of sheath knives. Instead of playing with ten fingers, he was using two knives. He always saved that for the finale or the encore, since that stunt effectively ended the usefulness of that particular keyboard. Another of his tricks was to play the organ upside down with one hand while dragging the instrument across the stage with the other hand. He never placed the forward edge of the organ back on the stage. He always let it fall back, since that produced a loud electronic crashing, splashing effect, which was a favourite of his. Through all of this, his comrades would stand on the other side of the stage, struggling to keep up with Emerson musically. They never quite made it. They didn't have the ability to anticipate him. So they had to react to what he was doing. To the average crowd this sounded fine, but to anyone who was familiar with music, it always sounded like they were two notes behind him, which they were."

"When Emerson, Lake and Palmer hit the Fillmore East stage, it looked as if the group could have been called The Nice Revisited. There was Emerson with his usual two-thirds of the stage, with Lake and Palmer sharing what space was left. The big difference was in the instruments Emerson had with him. On the extreme left side of the stage was his old Hammond, complete with its two keyboards and foot pedals. On top of that, however, was another keyboard which was attached to an entire bank of control boards, switches and patch cords. Crowning these various Frankenstein-ish things, you see flashing orange lights, which are, in fact, a digital readout. This is Keith Emerson's newest toy: a Moog synthesiser. Facing the Hammond, keyboard to keyboard and about three feet away, is the small organ. On another section of the stage is a grand piano, with yet another keyboard sitting on top. The extra keyboard is an electronic piano, judging from the sound of it. These were Emerson's toys and he used them to their utmost. In one song he played the Moog. He hit one note on the

43

Moog at the end of a passage on that instrument and made the note echo long enough that he could run from the Moog to the piano and take over there. The entire performance was a study in musical virtuosity."

"The major difference between The Nice and Emerson, Lake and Palmer is in the back-up. While Jackson and Davison of The Nice only reacted to Emerson's playing, Lake and Palmer anticipate his moves. They are behind him one-hundred percent. The singer for The Nice was Lee Jackson. His singing was good, but he only had one voice, so to speak. Whether he sang a ballad or a blues number, he sounded the same. When Lake sings, however, his voice changes to suit the music. He controls his voice to meet the emotion of the song. Lake makes up for everything that Jackson was missing. And he is not restricted to playing bass guitar, but also does a fair job with electric guitar and an acoustic guitar in one song. Carl Palmer plays the intricate sort of drum lines that were always missing in The Nice. His ease of intricacy matches what Emerson is doing perfectly. The drum solo which he does on 'Rondo', an old Nice number which Emerson chose to retain, is a thing of beauty. In concert, the group does almost all of its first album. But not every song is called by the same title as it is on the album. For example, elements of 'Tank' showed up in 'Knife-Edge', while part of 'The Three Fates' came out during 'The Barbarian'. As usual, Emerson steals from every possible source in his music. 'Lady Madonna' crept into at least two songs, and the encore which Emerson announced as a 1950s rock number called 'Nut Rocker' was in fact, Tchaikovsky's *Nutcracker* suite. Emerson's onstage tricks have carried over from The Nice. As always, he makes sure that his part of the stage will be the part that everyone is watching. He picks up the organ and drags it around, he drags it over to the amplifier to get feedback, he dances, he writhes, he jumps off the stage and into the audience, he forces unearthly noises from every instrument. Yet somehow, through all of that, you can't miss the fact that he is still playing some of the best keyboard music to be found anywhere."

It was reported in *Disc & Music Echo* in July 1971; "As far as this year is concerned, Emerson, Lake and Palmer could be the hardest-working band. They've done around one-hundred concerts (each at least two hours long) in about one-hundred-and-fifty days. Now their second album, *Tarkus*, is top in Britain, and success hasn't come by way of self-indulgence or ignoring the need to entertain audiences. If you like, ELP are "un-cool". They know exactly what they are going to play when they go on stage, and they put themselves into it. It's not strictly a policy, but they are doing things the way they feel they ought to be done."

Overall, as hard as they were working, things were going well for

ELP, and this period in their tenure was one that they would look back on favourably the following year. Palmer said of *Tarkus* in January 1972; "I prefer to think of it as being the first album that we cut as a band. We were so much together on those sessions and playing without any pressures, whereas our first album was more or less a proving point to initially show what we were capable of doing. On *Tarkus*, we did it." Lake told *New Musical Express* in July 1972; "Personally, I've always felt *Tarkus* was our best album collectively and so does Carl, but everyone's entitled to an opinion."

Following the release of *Tarkus*, ELP's next album was *Pictures At An Exhibition*. It came out in the UK in November 1971. It features part of their performance that was recorded at Newcastle City Hall on 26th March 1971. In March 2013, under the pseudonym of Rob Pieroni, an eyewitness posted online on the Steve Hoffman Forum:

"I was at the gig, still live locally. ELP played the City Hall and Keith played the Hall's pipe organ on *Pictures* on the UK tour previous to March '71, so they knew what they could expect when planning a live recording. The 'sssshh' from the audience at the start of the album was the general reaction to Greg saying 'we're recording tonight so please be quiet for the first part'; the organ was mic'd from the centre of the hall so it was always going to pick up anything ambient. I think we did okay. I'd love to hear again the rest of the gig, it was to the same quality of playing and if Mr Offord was recording should have been as well taped. The Hall historically has had a good acoustic track record, there's a couple of live tracks on the Small Faces *Autumn Stone* album."

"I'd dispute that the audience sound has been doctored but admit I am puzzled that all CD reissues so far haven't sonically joined up sides one and two of the vinyl. That much doesn't gel. I wrote the setlist out onto my programme that evening thus:

The Barbarian
Tarkus
(I wrote 'Tarkas', it wasn't released at that date, bloomin' southern accents)
Jeremy Bender
Knife-Edge
Pictures At An Exhibition
Take A Pebble (piano improvs included 2nd Bridge from the *Five Bridges* suite)
Rondo
Nut Rocker (encore)"

Billboard reviewed the album positively; "The trio's deftness in adapting serious music into contemporary idiom has really flowered with this performance. Some originals and Kim Fowley's 'Nut Rocker' is beautifully integrated." A local American newspaper called it "a very unusual, but enjoyable album". Another said; "Their interpretation of the Mussorgsky impressionistic classical work leaves you breathless... The best trio in rock today has taken a major and important step in their group development and the continuing evolvement of rock music as a form that can be effective as serious music."

A local Canadian paper considered; "The album is driven by Emerson's hectic keyboard work, though there is one pleasant lull for some acoustic guitar. And if it's often closer to shazam than symphony, at least this live recording reduces the pompousness of ELP's studio work and allows the performance to stand as a sometimes silly, sometimes amusing, conjurer's act."

The *Reading Evening Post* opined; "I have only recently become addicted to ELP and this record has got me hooked even further. It is the trio's interpretation of the classic suite by Mussorgsky. On first hearing I found myself comparing it unfavourably to the original, but you have to bear in mind that this is the young, modern interpretation. Really, ELP have taken over Mussorgsky's theme and woven their own characteristic sounds and style around it. Keith Emerson is, of course, faultless with his intricate keyboard work and once again he explores scores of sounds with his Moog. Carl Palmer is as heavy and as furious as ever, but the highlight for me was the quiet interlude with Greg on guitar and vocal in 'The Sage'. The album was recorded live at Newcastle City Hall and the reproduction is first class. This suite has been a highlight of the band's established act for a long time, so it could only really have been done before a crowd. This must be another hit for them."

Interestingly, the review draws attention to the fact that with *Pictures At An Exhibition*, not only was ELP's work going to be compared to their previous albums but also, to the original Mussorgsky piece. Whilst Emerson's playing of the main theme, 'Promenade', is melodically on point (faithful to the original) and indeed beautiful, thereafter, there is a lot to be said for listening to ELP's version as something in and of itself, rather than reaching frequently at how it perhaps compares to Mussorgsky's. Still though, that's the risk that any band takes when they do their own version of an existing piece of music. Besides, it's still fascinating to compare the two pieces.

There was much uncertainty regarding how ELP's recording should be released, if at all! There was initially an idea to release *Pictures At*

An Exhibition as the second ELP album following the success of their eponymous debut. However, it was felt that the length and classical nature of the piece was such that it would struggle to get radio play. There was also a feeling from ELP that to release *Pictures At An Exhibition* as their second album would be a risk to their reputation overall because they didn't want to be pigeonholed as a band whose main thing was classical music. They decided to focus on *Tarkus* as their choice of second album.

Lake explained; "There was talk of releasing the Newcastle City Hall recording as ELP's second album, but the record company was not convinced that an interpretation of a whole classical suite was going to sell, despite how it had gone down at our live performances. The idea was shelved for the time being, but after the success of our second album and tour, it was released in November 1971, reaching number three in the UK album charts. As well as *Pictures*, the album included the live encore of 'Nut Rocker', inspired by Kim Fowley's version of the march from Tchaikovsky's ballet, *The Nutcracker*."

Lester Bangs reviewed *Pictures At An Exhibition* in *Rolling Stone* in March 1972; "If there's one thing you've gotta give ELP, it's balls. Not only did they take one of the most staid standards from the annals of "serious" music and do it in an amped-up electronic version that must drive freaks wild, but they added their own elaborations and improvisations and lyrics as well. Compared to this, the conceit and tastelessness involved in Jon Lord's *Gemini Suite* or the *Concerto For Group And Orchestra* he and Deep Purple performed with the Royal Philharmonic were nothing, the modest work of quiet craftsmen. Emerson, Lake and Palmer are bombastic and tasteless and they probably know it, but tastelessness has never been far from the sense of fun at the core of rock 'n' roll, or bombast either, these days. Back in the days when people spent a lot of time sitting stiff-backed in drawing rooms and there were no child labour laws, Mussorgsky wrote a piano chart called *Pictures At An Exhibition*, which was later rearranged for full orchestra by Maurice Ravel, whose smash hit *Bolero* was (comparatively) recently covered by Jeff Beck. *Pictures* is basically a series of short compositions meant to describe some paintings hanging in the Louvre, I believe, and back in the Kennedy sixties before I got my sensibilities corrupted and attention span obliterated by The Beatles et al., it was one of my fave classical raves. If poor old Mussorgsky and Ravel can hear what Emerson, Lake and Palmer have done to their music, they are probably getting dry heaves in the void; speaking strictly as a fan of M & R and heretofore certified disdainer of E, L & P, however, I can say that I listened to it twice tonight, beating my fists on the floor and laughing, and I got my kicks."

"The proceedings, recorded live in England, begin with Mussorgsky's basic and conjunctive theme, the 'Promenade', played in a somewhat Bachic style, as if Keith Emerson were whacking away at the biggest pipe organ in the oldest church in Vienna. The 'Gnomes' theme from the original work, here credited to give such where it's due to (Mussorgsky/Palmer), enters abruptly to whistles and yells from the audience, swizzled out on Emerson's Mellotron or customised organ or whatever, with wah-wah counterpoint by Lake. After some strange, kinetic soloing, 'Promenade' returns with lyrics by Lake: 'Lead me from tortured dreams...'. You said it, brother. Because from this point I begin to lose track of Mussorgsky and get caught up in the ELP furore for the rest of the side. Beginning with a Lake compo called 'The Sage' that has about as much to do with *Pictures At An Exhibition* as ELP's lyrics do with the programmatic significance of the original piece, but it's vintage ELP anyway, except for one boring bit where Lake indulges himself in some gossamer Laurindo Almeidaisms. Luckily, however, they don't last long. A minute later and we're hit in the face: Whizz! Whirrr! Whee! It's a full-blown slashing, crashing, urping, burping electronic freakout and boy does the crowd eat it up, along with the 'Blues Variation' which follows and takes the side out in gales of applause and more space bleeps. But what's this? I look in the album jacket and I see one of Mussorgsky's original themes, 'The Old Castle', listed (and supposedly elaborated on a bit by Emerson). Well, he must have elaborated the thing clear to Aldebaran, because I hear nary a hint of 'The Old Castle' anywhere on this record. Come to think of it, the original piece also had a couple of sections called 'Tuileries' and 'Ballet Of Chicks In Their Shells' (a sexist fantasy about a troupe of danseuses vacationing at the Black Sea being devoured by giant clams) that aren't even mentioned here. Oh well, fuck it, ELP know what they're doing and there's no sense having any dross cluttering up an otherwise fine album."

"Side two begins with the 'Promenade' rendered stately as hell, heavy on the bass drum. They could play it at your high school graduation. Followed by a chart scripted by Mussorgsky completely without Limey and this time, called 'The Hut Of Baba Yaga', which in the original was about an old witch who went around snatching children and parboiling them for supper or some such. With such meaty subject matter, it stands to reason that it's done pretty much straight (except for the wah-wah Mellotron farts). Segueing into an ELP song called 'The Curse Of Baba Yaga' which for once seems to have some relation to Mussorgsky's themes, with a quick vocal that's almost impossible to catch and even quicker riffing — Keith Emerson really does know his axe inside and out, the Alvin Lee of Bach rock — surging back through the original 'Baba Yaga' theme and right up to 'The Great Gates Of Kiev'. And man, when those gates open you better have some waterwings, 'cause the whole grand sprawling mess that's Emerson, Lake and Palmer at their best comes gushing out: not only a reprise of Whizz! and Whirrr!, but also Boink!, Grrr!, Skizzrrlll!, feedback and applause falling together like the walls of the Red Sea right after Moses' troops tramped through, and, yep, more lyrics: 'They were sent from the gate... For life to be...' Be what? He leaves the line to trail off in the air. The tension is unbearable, and the audience is fairly seething. But suddenly, abruptly, we are treated to the coda vocal and it all comes clear, sort of: 'There's no end to my life... Death is life'. Hmmm, don't know if I like them lines, sounds kinda like Charles Manson to me. But don't let the seeming obscurity fool you, because that inference is part of the grand plan too: the encore is 'Nut Rocker'."

Did Bangs really need to negate the merits of Jon Lord's *Gemini Suite* and *Concerto For Group And Orchestra* when reviewing ELP's *Pictures At An Exhibition*? Both pieces stand as artistically worthwhile in their own right. Similarly, both ELP's *Pictures* and Deep Purple's *Concerto* stand as monumental landmarks in the careers of both bands; they are both live recordings that would be all too easy to overlook in both band's discographies but actually, they were both important (even if they are more niche than, for instance, the studio albums *Tarkus* and *Deep Purple In Rock*).

One of the most agreeable things, perhaps, that Bangs mentions in his review of *Pictures At An Exhibition* is that, for anyone not tremendously familiar with Mussorgsky's original piece, it is very easy to listen to ELP's version and not be absolutely certain of who composed which bits. It is testament to the quality of ELP's writing as in, they succeeded to continue the mood and character of the original piece into something that they made their own. It shouldn't come as a surprise though; both Emerson and Lake had always used classical music as a strong point of reference earlier in their careers.

With regards to the fact that ELP added a lot of their own ideas to their version of *Pictures At An Exhibition*, Emerson told *Beetle* in February 1974; "Even though they were written by us, they were inspired by Mussorgsky's original piece. 'Blues Variations' is really one of the phases of one of the movements in *Pictures* called 'The Old Castle'. The actual thing goes very slow and mournful, so I just made it into a shuffle so there was a blues variation on that particular thing. Then Greg had the idea of the minstrel singing underneath the castle, which was 'The Sage'. So it all related to that. We had to sort of put our own thing into that as well. We put some of our own *Pictures At An Exhibition* into Mussorgsky's *Pictures*

At An Exhibition".

He told *Circus* in March 1972; "When we started playing in England, *Pictures* was like a blueprint to get the group's musical direction together. Mainly just to get out a whole thing and play it together. We had to learn how to play together 'cause we hadn't really got a system of writing our own music. It takes a long time for musicians to understand each other's musical thinking and be able to sort of put them together. It's only since *Tarkus* that we really got into a good system of writing together, so *Pictures* was like a first stage. We played it all around England and people wanted it, so we decided to give it to them."

Upon being asked why out of all the classical pieces of music, he chose to do a full-blown adaptation of *Pictures At An Exhibition*, Emerson explained; "I liked it. I just liked the tune and I wanted to play it. It's as simple as that. I have a love for classical music and I like jazz as well. There aren't many rock bands I listen to. I spend about six months writing a piece of music of my own. So it's refreshing to me to play something else written by someone else, something which I like. I first heard *Pictures At An Exhibition* at the Royal Festival Hall performed by an orchestra and I came out of the concert thinking it was far out, 'I've got to play that'."

Along with the thought that went into setting up prior to the performance of *Pictures At An Exhibition*, Newcastle City Hall must have been a good choice of venue for acoustics. It was considered in *Circus* in March 1972; "One of the things the critics have praised most about the *Pictures* album is the sound quality; this is no accident. Poor reproduction is one of the major hazards of recording live."

Emerson told the journalist; "It's not easy to get a good sound. When we recorded *Pictures* in England, we spent all day just working on the sound system... *Pictures At An Exhibition* was recorded live because it contained a lot of improvisation. I get more of a buzz playing an improvisation live than playing it cold in the studio. I probably will do more live recording; it just takes a lot to get it together."

It is very plausible that the success of *Tarkus* gave all concerned the confidence to release *Pictures At An Exhibition* as an album in its own right. Overall, the period was an incredibly fruitful one for Emerson, Lake and Palmer.

4.
I've Seen Paupers As Kings

ELP took a break from touring in September 1971 to record new material for what would be their third studio album, *Trilogy*. It saw them going to London's Advision Studios with Eddy Offord on engineering duties. After doing more live performances over November and December, the band also utilised February and March 1972 to work on *Trilogy*.

Emerson stated that he was pleased that the material was notably different to *Tarkus*. With *Tarkus* having confirmed ELP's position commercially in 1971 and with *Pictures At An Exhibition* being seen as something of a side project, in 1972, ELP's *Trilogy* album moved somewhat away from the group's use of classical music influences.

To move away from such influences was certainly not to simplify the process of making an album — far from it, in fact! Lake considered that *Trilogy* was a difficult album to record due to how it was "such an accurate record". Palmer considered in later years that of all ELP's albums, *Trilogy* had the most number of overdubs on it due to the "enormous detail" in the song arrangements.

The drummer told *Hit Parader* in January 1972; "At first we were lumbered with that superstar trip and we had to fight very hard to overcome it. I know that from the beginning we were given a very good break but I can tell you we really had to prove ourselves. Thankfully, it seems as if we've been accepted but it doesn't stop there. Once you've been accepted, you can't slow down. That's the time you've really got to work harder, simply because there's so much more to fight for. Nowadays you've really got to stay on the ball, especially with all these new guys coming along."

Trilogy was released in July 1972 on Island Records. It got to number two in the UK and to number five on the Billboard 200. It appeared in the top ten in Denmark for four non-consecutive weeks (it peaked at number six there). *Billboard* advocated positively of the album on the basis of Emerson's "steady progression" on the Moog synthesiser.

Trilogy increased ELP's worldwide popularity. It included the track, 'Hoedown' — an arrangement of the Aaron Copland composition. It quickly became one of ELP's most popular songs live. With new material from the *Trilogy* album added into the setlist, ELP began to use less content from *Pictures At An Exhibition*. Material from the latter went on to become the stuff of ELP encores in later years. *Trilogy* did well in the US and the song, 'From The Beginning', made ELP's music accessible to a wider audience. It was released as a single and it got to number thirty-nine in the US. Lake said of when he wrote the song, "I just felt an inspiration to do it, and it flowed through me in a natural way. My hands fell upon these very unusual chords... It was kind of a gift."

Hipgnosis, who had already created covers for The Nice, and most notably, for Pink Floyd, designed the artwork. The interior of the original gatefold sleeve features a photomontage of ELP in Epping Forest. The front cover of the album was the first of ELP's to feature their faces; Emerson asserted that this was a deliberate decision rather than a product of coincidence.

The graphic advertising *Trilogy* in the UK music press at the time featured a quote from Emerson: "I've never really stopped to consider our place in contemporary music. We've never put our music alongside anyone else's to see the difference. We play what we believe in and hope others will enjoy it." The effective choice of quote provided a hint as to not only the band's identity and approach, but the record's too.

Trilogy was reviewed in the *Coventry Evening Telegraph*; "The trio sound like an orchestra once keyboard master Keith Emerson gets under way on Moog synthesiser, mini-Moog, organ and piano. There is variety indeed throughout, with 'Abaddon's Bolero' based on the Ravel piece — a real tour de force. It follows the line of adaptations of classical pieces Emerson has pursued since The Nice. This LP is aptly titled and Greg Lake's vocals and Carl Palmer's percussion add to the attack."

It was reviewed in the *Buckinghamshire Examiner*; "The combined musical talents of Emerson, Lake and Palmer are more than capable of producing work that is not only musically competent but original and inventive too. But somewhere along the line they have got tied up in themselves, and the music has become too stale. There is a little of the originality that Keith Emerson displayed with The Nice. Perhaps not surprisingly, the band has all but been taken over by Emerson, with his organ, piano and Moog synthesiser. But listening to his performance on the band's new album, *Trilogy*, it seemed it has all been heard before. In fact, on the first side, there is little of note except 'From The Beginning' — dominated by Greg Lake's acoustic guitar work. In fairness, the poor first side is balanced by a good second side, which includes the long title track 'Trilogy'. The only other tracks are 'Living Sin' and 'Abaddon's Bolero'. The band has been together for some time now — and *Trilogy* must be a turning point for them. They should either change their musical direction or split up, because they are offering nothing new to their followers."

And in the *Reading Evening Post*; "I received this record just before I left on holiday and in those two weeks (holidays are always too short) it has jumped into the album charts, so it is obviously already a hit with ELP fans. It is up to the usual high standard we have all come to expect from this trio, but I felt like it fell a little short of *Tarkus* and *Pictures At An Exhibition*. It doesn't have a strong theme like those two, and at times I felt it was more of an exercise in what sort of sounds Emerson could get out of his Hammond and Moog. But once I forced that "treasonable" thought out of my mind, I quite enjoyed the album, particularly Greg Lake's smooth 'From The Beginning'."

Just prior to the release of *Trilogy*, it is clear that the complexity of the music was such that the band were reluctant to perform it on stage. *The Miami News* reported in April 1972; "Either Emerson, Lake and Palmer are average musicians taking us all for a ride, or else they're extraordinary showmen capable of turning an audience into a mass of dancing, clapping fans. As a result of their performance last Friday night, my guess would be the latter. Emerson, Lake and Palmer have been heralded by the publicity men as a supergroup. Their three albums have tended to agree with this label, but excellent live performances truly make a supergroup stand out from the rest. Although they were plagued with bass cable problems, Emerson, Lake and Palmer convinced the audience at Miami Beach Convention Hall that they are a musical power to be reckoned with."

"Once Emerson, Lake and Palmer took the stage, 6,500 pairs of eyes were on them. Immediately, Keith Emerson slammed into his electric organ, producing loud, (very) unusual noises. It was only into the second song that Emerson began to give the audience the show they'd been waiting for. Playing the huge Moog with one hand and the organ with the other, Emerson got into some sounds that were truly incredible — all the while peering at the audience like a mad scientist to see what its reaction was. Then, taking a portable Moog board, Emerson jumped into the audience, emitting machine-gun-like noises. Jumping back onto the stage and landing into a somersault, Emerson left the audience speechless.

A few songs later in the evening's only bad spot, Greg Lake's bass cable broke, causing a five-minute delay."

"After the intermission, the group launched into 'Tarkus', the title cut from the second album. Again, the versatility displayed by Emerson, Lake and Palmer totally astounded the audience. In an abrupt change of style, Lake led off the beautiful 'Lucky Man' on acoustic guitar. Despite shouts from the audience for new material, the band continued to play older songs, 'Take A Pebble' among them. Finally, the group played excerpts from its celebrated version of Mussorgsky's *Pictures At An Exhibition*. Augmented by Moog, organ, bass and drums, the selections had a sound that would make Mussorgsky turn over in his grave. An encore featuring a Carl Palmer drum solo with thrashing gongs and Keith Emerson riding the organ across the stage and finally kicking it over ended the night's music. Emerson, Lake and Palmer perform a show that is exceptional in all respects, musical, theatrics, except one — feeling. Put a little feeling or emotion into their songs and they would be superb."

The review highlights the way in which the songs from *Trilogy* did not lend themselves to being performed live. Not only that, but the audience clearly noticed the absence of newer material. It wouldn't have necessarily made for a bad gig but it was certainly something that would go on to inform ELP's approach to their next album. In particular, the issue with the band not being able to perform material from *Trilogy* live is something that was picked up on by more than one critic.

The *Detroit Free Press* considered in April 1972; "If Emerson, Lake and Palmer's music is not top-notch, their performance is. The excitement of ELP is what makes them fun. As musicians, they have an unfortunate sameness to their performances that gives the music a slightly stale flavour. *Tarkus* for example, is old hat by now, and even their treatment of *Pictures At An Exhibition* is more lobotomy than adaptation. A version of 'Bolero' promised for Monday night never materialised because of faulty tape equipment, hence *Pictures*. And the encores were 'Nut Rocker' and 'Rondo', both old, filled with the visual fireworks which the group is so good at. One wished, though, that ELP had the musical spark shown by the concert's opening act, John McLaughlin and the Mahavishnu Orchestra."

Tarkus was still proving to be good material for performance though. Lake called it "an aggressive piece of music" and went on to state; "That's the simplest way to impress a feeling on the audience. Light sounds, you can ignore, but if Mars the God of War is making noise while you're eating dinner, you'll notice."

After the release of *Trilogy*, ELP toured Europe and the US, playing to sold-out venues. By the beginning of 1973, ELP had secured commercial success in both the UK and the US. They were also given a strong response from fans in Europe. Lake told *New Musical Express* in July 1972; "Receptions have been great. In Italy, they were just completely amazed, and in Berlin, I thought we'd started another bloody war. You can always tell when it is going to be a big one in Europe. They turn out the army, the riot squad and the police — it was a bit like that in Germany. It's only when you come out to places like this and begin to travel these distances, you really appreciate how small the world really is and how little difference there is between nationalities. We mostly all want the same things and the only barrier is language, which we can at least break down with music. You can't really analyse your own success, but I think one of the reasons we have been accepted so broadly is that we don't strike attitudes or attempt to indoctrinate people. Occasionally, we present an idea, but we don't brainwash people."

In July 1972, *New Musical Express* reported on a performance that ELP did in Switzerland; ""Fingers" is, of course, the focal point of the action on stage and there he is on his back with the organ on top of him and musically raping the contraption. He thrashes the keyboard, rocks and rides it across the stage and finally hurls it about, raising great clouds of blanco to smother the hordes of photographers and all the time the most amazing sounds are happening. He has the damn thing in pain. Lesser musicians than Carl Palmer and Greg Lake might be swamped by his amazing virtuosity, but they are not."

"They follow him at every twist and turn of his switching styles, and offhand I cannot think of another percussionist in any contemporary group who could match him as Palmer does and even come out on top. Greg does much to provide the perfect balance between them and still gets his justifiable acclaim during solos with 'Lucky Man' and 'Take A Pebble'."

"All three together provide a unique identity which far transcends any individual. I cannot think of another group who get so many different styles into their act or indeed of musicians capable of adapting to them. During one piece of incredible dexterity, Emerson turned to honky-tonk piano, blues, jazz, classic, boogie woogie and even threw in a touch of the 1812 Overture. All my favourite items were there from *Tarkus*, *Pictures At An Exhibition*, plus two new items from their new album, *Trilogy*: 'The Endless Enigma' and 'Hoedown'. Then, of course, the finale to end all finales, 'Rondo' — which is a national anthem — although ELP are currently providing a recorded classical piece called *Church Windows* to send the customers home in a more tranquil mood."

"Despite this, I might add, this particular audience refused to go for almost fifteen minutes, during which they set up a non-stop roar of

The ELP Story - *A Time and a Place*

approval for music received and understood. They cheered when Greg switched to acoustic. They cheered when Carl used a gong. They cheered when Keith switched from piano to organ. They might very well have cheered if he had blown his nose."

Before moving on to other dates in the west, the band went to Japan. Upon their arrival there, they did a number of interviews to promote the upcoming shows. In one that was recorded on camera, when asked what they would be doing after the interview, Lake, with a sense of humour about the whole thing, said they would be doing more interviews. It is clear that the band were in good spirits. When the interviewer asked if the group had a message for the viewers at home, an impish-looking Emerson giggled as Palmer put his arm around him and told the camera; "He had a bracelet stolen at the airport and he would like it back, so anyone who's looking in that stole his bracelet, he needs the money."

In July 1972, Chris Welch wrote for *Melody Maker*: "A full-scale riot stopped Emerson, Lake and Palmer's show at a massive baseball stadium in Osaka, Japan on Monday night. As Keith Emerson swept into their perennial rave-up on 'Rondo', thousands of yelling teenagers hurling firecrackers leaped over barriers and charged the stage. Girls and boys jumped on the stage and grabbed Greg Lake who was rescued by security men. Police clubbed down fans but were overwhelmed and meanwhile the power supply went dead. Later the police demanded the show be stopped. Carl Palmer was halfway through his drum solo when Keith and Greg fled the stage. Carl threw down his sticks and jumped into another car that raced through the seething mob. For half-an-hour, angry and disappointed fans kept up chants for the group to return but it was impossible and a furious Greg Lake said later, 'There just wasn't enough security. We couldn't play any more'."

"It was a shame that Emerson, Lake and Palmer's first visit to Japan ended in chaos and disappointment. On Saturday night at the Tokyo baseball stadium, 35,000 fans cheered them as they battled through a rainstorm. Osaka was to have been the climax to a week of promotion of British rock in Japan. But a special firework display had to be abandoned and Keith Emerson hadn't even time to hurl a symbolic dagger at his equipment. Sprays of rainwater flew off Carl Palmer's shimmering symbols as ELP made their Tokyo debut in the typhoon downpour. But the rain could not stop ELP and fans gave them a hero's welcome while live TV pictures were relayed to the city. In a temperature of ninety degrees, Carl and Greg — soaked to the skin — did their best to give a musical as well as spectacular performance. By a miracle of co-operation between Japanese

I've Seen Paupers As Kings

workmen and ELP's team of eight technicians, the sound was fine and the lighting and power kept working. Fans huddled under umbrellas as black clouds scudded over the pitch. Carl Palmer grimly played on while the worst of the downpour came during his solo on 'Rondo'. Greg and Keith sheltered but Palmer played on sticks flashing around his twelve-drum kit, his face contoured with effort when he hit the tom-toms, the effect was like a motorboat racing through choppy seas."

"Later, Carl collapsed in his hotel bedroom, and Keith was violently sick in the car that took them back to the Tokyo Hilton. All week, Keith had been worried about the open-air concert, particularly the effects of humidity on his Moog synthesiser, which he knew would go out of tune. Just an hour before the concert, he telephoned the inventor, Bob Moog, in America for advice, but could get no reply. The delicate synthesiser, vital to ELP's act, was kept cool with a battery of electric fans. Keith fought to keep it under control and just managed to get through a phenomenal version of *Pictures At An Exhibition*. Said Keith, 'It's like being an astronaut on the moon and you've got a big problem. The only guy that can help you is at mission control thousands of miles away.' The band had been looking forward with eager excitement to the gig in a country just opening up to rock music. Although record sales are not comparable with America, the success of appearances by Jethro Tull, Free and ELP in one week augers as well for the future. ELP's arrival in the country was greeted by near riot at the airport and when they finally got to the baseball stadium, the atmosphere was quite emotional, like the arrival of warriors from some distant battle point. Fans let off fireworks and rockets but generally remained good-natured."

"A car drove ELP on stage and they came out in kimonos to bow, which caused a roar of approval from the Japanese. Their opener, 'Hoedown', a boisterous number from their *Trilogy* album, proved an excellent way of hitting the audience. ELP are into drawing maximum response. The combination of brilliant arrangements, executed with sheer professionalism, provided a heady mixture for the excitable fans, and when Keith waved a massive samurai sword, it sent a physical shock through the crowd. When he stamped it into the keyboard, there was near pandemonium. But apart from the dagger-throwing, organ gymnastics, and erotic motions with his Moog ribbon controller, there was a lot of fine music for the discerning to enjoy. Greg Lake was luckiest in being able to put over songs like 'Lucky Man' during the less hectic moments. Keith played superbly aggressive piano on 'Take A Pebble', which emphasised that he is still thinking hard about musical progression, which is the main object of the band. Carl's drumming was phenomenal when he got a chance to play and wasn't interrupted by typhoons and riots. The arrangements were not always as accurately played as is expected of ELP but this was due to a long layoff and the appalling conditions at the gigs. On Tuesday, the group were due to leave for America to start a four-week tour and said Carl Palmer: 'After this, I can't wait to get there'."

It was reported in the *Harrow Observer* in October 1972; "Fantastic. An incredible musical spectacle. Undoubtedly the most talented group of the decade — that, in my opinion, is the only way to describe Emerson, Lake and Palmer. And if you think I'm exaggerating, ask the 20,000 pop fans who crowded into the Oval for the *Melody Maker* poll awards concert on Saturday, and I am sure they will agree. Keith Emerson is a brilliant pianist, organist and one of the few who can really play the synthesiser. Carl Palmer is a drummer who can play a set of twenty drums for two hours without missing a beat. Greg Lake is a brilliant guitarist who provides the vocals. However, vocally the group is nothing, and to be quite frank, Greg Lake has no depth to his voice, which is the only weak link in what is otherwise a musically perfect group. Their music is very much influenced by the classical composers. Some is tuneful, other numbers are based on a pulsating beat, which can send an audience into a hypnotic trance. They played for two hours on Saturday, during which time, two giant model hedgehogs on either side of the stage puffed smoke from their nostrils. The end of the act was incredible. The stage was immersed in orange smoke, Carl Palmer used microphones for drumsticks and Keith Emerson managed to get his Moog synthesiser playing as if a complete orchestra was on stage."

By hedgehogs, the reviewer was undoubtedly referring to the Tarkus models! Of Greg Lake's singing, it is difficult to comment because live performances are always demanding on a singer (it is rumoured that this is why Lake was chewing gum in ELP's iconic performance at the California Jam in 1974 — more on that performance later!). What really stands out in the latter report is the fact that so much stamina and accuracy was apparent in ELP's live performance.

In November 1972, the *Birmingham Daily Post* reported on ELP's performance at Birmingham's Odeon; "Emerson, Lake and Palmer gave an enthusiastic and exhilarating performance, demonstrating why so many people are talking favourably about their individual style. The energy they put into a hard night's work said much for their stamina and the regard they have for the packed houses that greet them wherever they play. Keith Emerson, with his various keyboard instruments, and Birmingham-born Carl Palmer on drums, particularly showed why one-night stands can be so gruelling for a travelling band. Emerson even ventured into the audience

I've Seen Paupers As Kings

in the early stages, trailing with him part of the Moog synthesiser. Their music is the type that no one can like all the time and the softer numbers came as a welcome analgesic to some of the ear-shattering sounds with which they are more associated. Much of their music is reminiscent of the sadly defunct Nice band. Greg Lake's singing frequently suffered against the organ and drums in arrangements that seemed more like a battle than accompaniment. Highlights of the evening were the gentle songs. 'Take A Pebble' and 'Lucky Man', in which Lake's singing had a chance to show its true colours, and *Pictures At An Exhibition*. Predictably, they played 'Nut Rocker' for an encore, with Palmer's drum, gong and bell solo bringing strenuous response from the audience. An exciting night at the Odeon."

It was reported in the *Acton Gazette* in December 1972; "Emerson, Lake and Palmer have never had a hit single and you have never seen them on *Top Of The Pops* but it was like a full-scale invasion when their fans swarmed to see them at Hammersmith Odeon on Saturday. Successful as the other recent concerts have been at this ever-improving music venue, they never even approached the popularity of ELP. This fast-growing cult group have gained their following not by elaborate stage acts, flashy clothes or expensive publicity stunts, but simply by being three very talented musicians. It is very difficult to be indifferent about Emerson, Lake and Palmer — you either like them or you loathe them. It certainly did not take long to discover how the wall-to-wall audience at the Odeon felt about them. They stamped, shouted, whistled and clapped both in recognition at the start of each number, and in appreciation at the end of it."

"The stage itself looked set for a scene out of some bizarre science-fiction play, with banks of speakers and amplifiers, flashing lights and all the twinkling electronic paraphernalia that surrounds organist extraordinaire Keith Emerson. There were even a couple of giant model monsters, which breathed fire and smoke at various points during the proceedings. To their fans, their unique brand of futuristic music is as far removed from the ordinary "pop" scene as it is from Beethoven or Bach. Drawing a lot of its influence from jazz, it has the same indescribable compulsion for those who like and a complete incomprehension for those who do not."

"The star of the evening, if there was one, was undoubtedly Keith Emerson, who flitted between organ, Moog, piano and back to organ again, like some demonic electrician, throwing switches and pushing in plugs to produce the most incredible sounds. At the same time, the drummer Carl Palmer hammered away as if his life depended on it, using a few extra percussive nick-nacks such as two enormous Chinese gongs, cylindrical chimes and even a Moog drum. It may not really be music in the purest sense, but as entertainment, you only had to hear the deafening shouts for more at the close of the show if you wanted proof of its effect on the audience."

In March 1972, Emerson had told *Circus* about the theatrical elements of being on stage; "I've gone on and I've played and I've not done any theatrics at all and it's gone down just as well, so I have a choice really of doing it or not doing it. It all started (the whole thing wasn't planned) out of being exhilarated onstage and reaching a point where the music was no longer sufficient to reach a climax. There weren't notes good enough to go above what you wanted to do and that's the point where I started going into this other medium, the visual side. The way I look on the stage act now is creation and destruction. The visual side of the act does become destructive art. The fact that we're creating right from the start can only reach a certain peak musically. That's why I'm sort of into destructive art; that's what Pete Townsend is into anyway. It's a whole sort of thing with The Who. I think there's a place for destructive art in music."

"Music is generally a release and whatever way a musician chooses to do it, whether visually or musically, I don't think it matters as long as the music comes out the same and everything I do which can be considered as a theatrical does a certain function in the music. The fact that I choose to ride an organ across the stage has a function in the music. I could get the same effect if I stood there and shook the instrument, because what is happening is the reverberation unit in the back is crashing and making a big explosive sound. I could do the same thing by standing in one place and rocking the organ, but I get the same effect out of riding it across the stage, so why not do it?"

"Using knives in the act came from when The Nice were doing 'America' and in 'America' (on *Ars Longa Vita Brevis*) I wanted to hold down two notes and sustain a fifth while I was playing another organ. I started out by using pegs, just wooden things to hold down the keys. Then I thought I could do the same thing with knives and if I'm playing 'America', the music from *West Side Story*, then the knives have a definite part in it, being connected with the film and the gang fights. So I thought, 'yes, it has a place here', and then I used to take the knives out of the keyboard and throw them on the floor; and then probably one night I decided to throw them at the cabinets. It has a place in the music. I mean, if I rode an organ across the stage and there wasn't anything coming out of it, that would be ridiculous."

The journalist conducting this interview mentioned how "one critic in England said that listening to a live record of Emerson, Lake and Palmer is even more satisfying than seeing them, because when you attend their concerts, too many visuals attract your attention and detract from the music". ELP's performance at London's Oval cricket ground was reviewed in *Circus* in January 1973; "As the crowd roared their approval, the group raced from backstage, launching immediately into 'Hoedown', the upbeat, good-humoured number from their recent *Trilogy* LP, and the crowd was on its feet. Without hesitation, the group jumped immediately into 'Tarkus', and simultaneously pulled off the biggest feat in the history of rock wizardry. Two mammoth armadillo tanks appeared on both sides of the stage, bellowing replicas of the figures on the *Tarkus* cover. The metal dragons breathed clouds of smoke, and, as the show thundered to its climactic high point, the tanks thundered an ear-deafening barrage, driving fans into a wild frenzy of excitement and jubilation. Keith pounded the piano as 'Take A Pebble' echoed from the massive multi-toned speakers, and Greg Lake brought down the house with his excellent acoustic guitar work on 'Lucky Man'."

"But with the advent of *Pictures At An Exhibition*, off the LP of the same name, the crowd watched in absolute amazement as Carl Palmer's drum solo threatened to pop the sliver of sun out of the darkening sky. In a fury, Carl hurled himself at the drum kit, battering the cymbals and destroying the gongs. The *Tarkus* tanks belched forth their deafening roar as London's last great rock concert of the season shrieked to its end — and ELP proved once again that they remain the world's greatest rock band, upholding their title of Britain's Best Band, (the title they won last year) and taking on the title of World's Best Band as well. As the last fans wearily straggled home, ELP slowly unwound backstage, gathering the remains of their shattered instruments with them. Each clutched at their golden trophies: top group, British and International; Emerson's tribute as the top keyboard man; Palmer's trophy as top drummer; Lake's souvenir as the world's most accomplished producer; ELP as the top pop arrangers; and finally the shared award, Keith Emerson and Greg Lake taking honours as the world's top composers."

After doing the tour to support *Trilogy*, ELP began work on new material that would further blend classical and rock influences. With their commercial profile growing ever higher, it made sense to take more control from a business perspective and as a result, ELP launched their own record company in March 1973.

ELP had become frustrated with Atlantic Records. It was felt that they were not getting involved enough when and where it mattered. ELP, along with their manager Stewart Young, decided to form their own record company. Collectively, they purchased an abandoned ABC cinema in Fulham, West London. They converted it into a rehearsal room and a company headquarters, which they later named, Manticore Records.

Named after the character from Persian mythology that was referred to on *Tarkus*, Manticore was operated by the band, along with their manager. Young had only been managing ELP since 1972 (having taken over the role from the band's previous management team, John Gaydon and David Enthoven). He had never managed a band before. Like his father before him, he worked as a chartered accountant. That had all changed when ELP walked into his father's office seeking tax advice.

"Greg mentioned the idea of the label to me in late 1972," Young recalled. "I was excited. This was at the time when the music business was really just starting and it was exciting to think about starting a record label that would be artist-driven — it was a partnership between Emerson, Lake and Palmer and myself."

Manticore's releases supported artists associated with the progressive music scene in Italy, UK singer-songwriters and some accessible funk rock with good potential for the American market. ELP were actively involved in the signings. "We really liked bands like PFM, Stray Dog, Banco, Keith Christmas, Pete Sinfield, and we wanted to get them heard," Emerson explained.

"We set up Manticore to try and make the entire record process as good as it could be," Lake said. "We were also aware of a number of artists who we knew were having problems getting their music released and getting a record deal. We thought that by setting up our label, we could control things a lot better and also help out some of the other artists we admired."

In April 1973, Atlantic promoter, Mario Medious, who had worked with ELP since their first album, was brought in to serve as the president of Manticore. The decision was made on the basis that ELP didn't have the time to do the job themselves. Atlantic handled distribution duties.

Regarding the emergence of Manticore, the journalist writing for *New Musical Express* in March 1973 considered; "This is, of course, an ELP venture. It has now grown into a record company in its own right but was originally set up to protect the band's interests and allow them to concentrate on the more creative areas unhindered by the hassles of contracts, tax and general economics. It's a shrewd move, but based on sensible rather than avaricious motives. Despite this, Lake still admits one has to be something of a businessman these days to be a successful rock musician, although there's almost a contradiction in terms — between the hustler and the artist, the schemer and the dreamer." To which Lake was quoted; "I know a lot of rock musicians who are getting a really bad deal financially and in terms of their careers. Sadly, if you don't look after your interests, nobody else will. Now I see less and less of the business side of it because it's all being taken care of."

Lake said in March 1974; "We created our own company because the record label we were with before wanted an album from us every six months, whether we were ready to do one or not. So our creative energies were being motivated not from within ourselves, but from people who were making money from us. Art should come from the love of wanting to create. So now we work at our own pace, and all of us like it a lot better."

He had told *The Daily Mirror* in October 1972; "One of the most difficult periods of my life was earlier this year when I realised all of a sudden we had nobody to compete with. The three of us are good and the group is better than any of us. But I've learned that every door you walk through, there's always another door. And baby, you've got to keep pushing."

Although Lake's comment could be considered crass or arrogant, the fact is that by this point, ELP had achieved so much in such a relatively short space of time. Not only did they have a strong sense of self-belief in what they could achieve as a band, but there was a strong awareness between them that potentially, they could achieve even more.

Emerson, Lake and Palmer had all tasted success before they got together.

Keith Emerson with Brian "Blinky" Davison, David O'List and Lee Jackson. In July 1968, as part of The Nice.

(Tony Gale, Pictorial Press Ltd / Alamy Stock Photo)

Greg Lake performing with King Crimson on *Top Of The Pops*, 25th March 1970.

(Tony Gale, Pictorial Press Ltd / Alamy Stock Photo)

Carl Palmer in August 1968 with The Crazy World Of Arthur Brown.

(Tony Gale, Pictorial Press Ltd / Alamy Stock Photo)

Keith Emerson, Greg Lake and Carl Palmer during the first public performance of ELP at Plymouth Guildhall on 23rd August 1970.

(Tony Byers / Alamy Stock Photo)

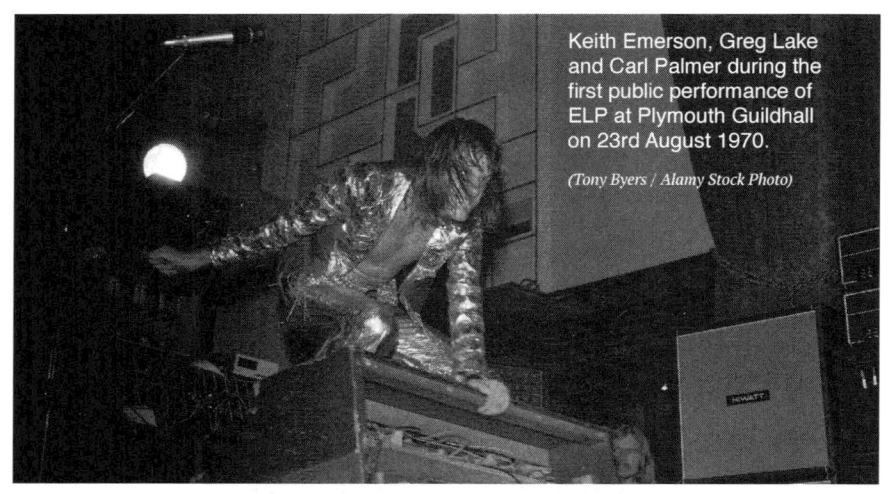

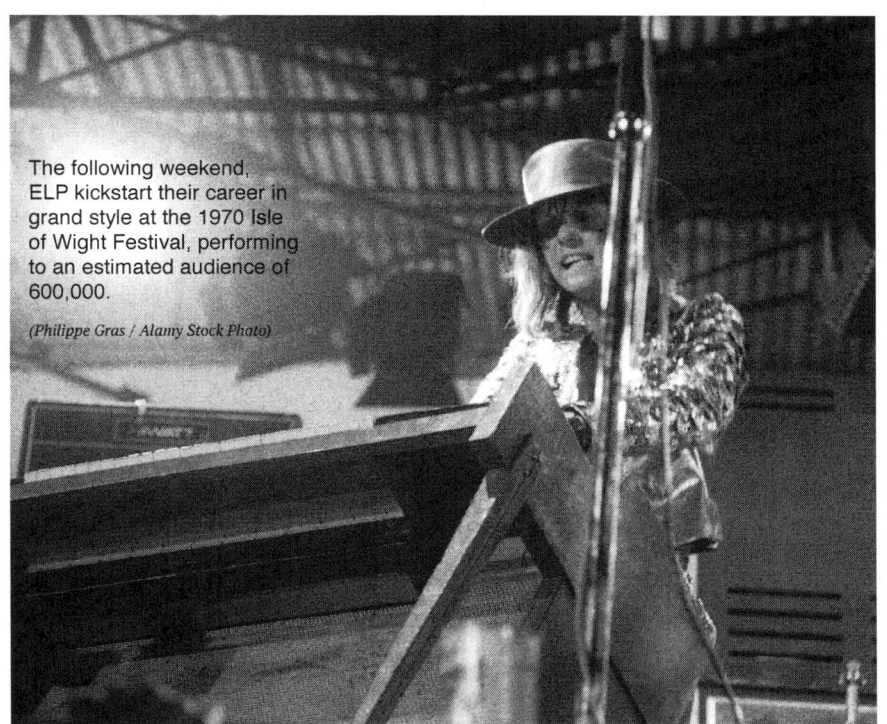

The following weekend, ELP kickstart their career in grand style at the 1970 Isle of Wight Festival, performing to an estimated audience of 600,000.

(Philippe Gras / Alamy Stock Photo)

Within a year of their formation, ELP were collecting accolades. Here they are at the
Melody Maker Awards, 16th September 1971.

(World Image Archive / Alamy Stock Photo)

Keith Emerson receiving a gold record from Minister of State for the Arts, Norman St John Stevas. In 1974, for *Brain Salad Surgery*. *(Marka/Press Holland / Alamy Stock Photo)*

On tour at the height of their success. *(Pictorial Press Ltd / Alamy Stock Photo)*

ELP's success afforded Keith the luxury of indulging in his passion for fast cars and motorbikes.
(Marka/Press Holland / Alamy Stock Photo)

30th June 1977, at the Columbia Coliseum in South Carolina, USA.

(Philip Buonpastore / Alamy Stock Photo)

The final ELP show took place at the High Voltage Festival in London's Victoria Park, 25th July 2010.

(Lee Milward)

Carl Palmer continues to fly the flag. Here he is during his Remembering Keith And The Music Of ELP tour, at the Molson Canadian Studio at Hamilton Place, Ontario, Canada, 8th June 2016. Greg Lake passed away six months later. Carl currently tours under the Carl Palmer's ELP Legacy moniker. *(Brent Perniac/AdMedia/ZUMA Wire/Alamy Live News)*

5.
You Could Be Anything

Not only many fans, but ELP themselves often asserted that the era of the *Brain Salad Surgery* album was one of the strongest for the band. "We were still ascending when we made *Brain Salad Surgery*," said Emerson. "We were enjoying a sensational amount of success, and I suppose we felt as if we could do anything — and we certainly tried. Musically, lyrically and visually, we really went for it." He considered that it was a "step forward from the past" that "represented the camaraderie of the band at the time".

Lake said in later years that it was "the last original, unique ELP album". And indeed, at the time, he keenly defended the band against the accusation that their music was pretentious: "Pretentious? I can't figure out why people keep saying that. We don't aim at it. We try our hardest and best because people pay a lot to see us and hear us. But sometimes we forget we're playing to non-musicians who often don't understand. People, however, especially American people, tend to investigate. We demand effort and we demand investigation. People sometimes resent it and call us pompous. We don't try to blind them, but the music does take some time. I'm happy for that. Because what takes longer, lasts longer... The most important thing is that we spent more time on this record than ever before. The reason for that is that we're concerned with being fresh and new and concerned with developing a style different from the first few albums. If you can isolate any differences on this one, well, it's more soulful. More raw ELP. We spent less time working on the technical structure of the thing and tried more for a natural flow. I think soulful's the word, though not necessarily soul."

"*Brain Salad Surgery* is the group at the pinnacle of its powers," said Palmer. "It's very well recorded and it was definitely one of our most creative periods. If I had to choose one of our albums, that would be the one. It's probably the most inventive album we made, but you don't realise that at the time you're making it as you're so wrapped up in it. And you never know quite how it will turn out."

And indeed, morale within the band seemed to be in a good place at the time. So much so that the group dynamics provided a comfortable space in which the three individual members could be fully creative. "There are two ways of expressing yourself as a musician," Lake told *New Musical Express* in March 1973. "One is to go for what you want and the other is to become the music of a group of people. If you do it on your own, you won't get the fusion or the flash that you can get out of a band, but you can't have your own way the whole time. To me, it seems if I play with two other people, I have to compromise, but in the long run, between us, we'll come up with more good music. Also, we're very fortunate because in the band, we all always listen to each other's ideas, so none of us gets inhibited in bringing something up. You know the others will listen, so you can play it with all your heart and conviction."

"It may sound corny," he added. "But the only ambition I have, and I'm sure it's shared by the rest of the band, is to extend as far as possible people's emotions through music, care and production. You can stretch them as far as your skill will allow and that's basically all there is to aim for. I'm not really into anything else, and I devote my life to it. If I wasn't doing it with this band, then it'd be with somebody else."

Brain Salad Surgery was recorded between June and September at Olympic and Advision Studios. It was mixed in October 1973 at George Martin's AIR Studios in London. As was the case with all of ELP's previous albums, their fourth was produced by Lake. It was released in November 1973 on their own label, Manticore Records. It was distributed by Atlantic Records. The album cover was designed by H.R. Giger. *Brain Salad Surgery* continued to support ELP's commercial success. It got to number two in the UK and to number eleven in the US. To support the album, ELP embarked on their largest world tour thus far — the one that included a headlining spot at the California Jam Festival in 1974.

ELP had started work on new material towards the end of 1972. Lake explained in an interview, that *Trilogy* had been recorded via the use of twenty-four-track machines and, as a result, featured too many overdubs that made the music very difficult to recreate well for live performance. A decision was therefore made to make an album that could comfortably be performed on stage.

"Music technology was really expanding," Lake explained. "Tape recorders were going from eight-track to twenty-four-track. We took advantage of the new possibilities and did a lot of overdubbing. But being a three-piece band, when we played it (*Trilogy*) live on tour, it didn't really sound as good as the record, so we made sure we could perform the next album live before we had even recorded it."

With the rehearsal facilities being a former cinema, it allowed ELP to alternate between playing live and then writing more material after assessing how it all played out. The band's Manticore Cinema in Fulham had plenty of space for them to set their gear up to replicate the setup of playing a live show.

It was during the writing sessions around late 1972/early 1973 that the first two tracks for *Brain Salad Surgery* began to take shape. One of them was the first movement of the epic 'Karn Evil 9'. The other was an adaptation of the fourth movement from Alberto Ginastera's Piano Concerto No.1.

Emerson said of writing 'Karn Evil 9'; "In between going back home from tour, mowing the lawn and saying 'hi' to the wife and kids, I'm not sure how I managed to write all this down. But I wrote it on manuscript paper and presented it to Greg and Carl. The first part of '1st Impression' used a lot of counterpoint and that worked well. Occasionally we used to make music up from blues jams, which could be fun, but I didn't always think that it was satisfactory."

Lake enthused that Emerson's music was "a perfect platform" upon which the lyrics could be added; "There's a character, like a ringmaster, who says, 'Welcome back, my friends, to the show that never ends'. It's slightly cold. 'We're so glad you could attend, come inside, come inside…' There's a wry smile that goes with it."

At nearly half-an-hour long, 'Karn Evil 9' consists of three movements. Originally, the first movement had to be split into two parts across sides one and two of the vinyl record. Although the original Atlantic CD remained loyal to the division of the suite, later releases have presented it as a cohesive piece. It combines inspiration from both rock and classical music. In terms of structure, the first and third movements are split up by a distinctive instrumental passage.

'Karn Evil 9' was initially intended to be an instrumental piece. This ultimately didn't emerge to be the case though. Lake wrote the lyrics for the first movement. To assist in writing the lyrics for the third movement, he brought in lyricist Peter Sinfield. Lake had worked with him before when he was in King Crimson. Sinfield recalled, "I was halfway through making a solo album when Greg called me to say that Manticore wanted to release it. The catch was that he wanted me to collaborate on lyrics for a long piece that had begun to take shape." Sinfield felt that the music Emerson had written reminded him of a carnival and he came up with the title 'Karn Evil 9' on such basis.

The sped-up and altered voice in the second movement and the "computer" voice in the third movement were made by Emerson — they were his only vocal contribution to the trio's repertoire. In order to create the "computer" voice, Emerson ran his voice through the Moog's ring modulator.

As far back as 1971, Emerson had been thinking about recording an adaptation of the fourth movement of Ginastera's Piano Concerto No.1. He was still a member of The Nice when he had first heard the piece and it had stayed with him since. It wasn't until Palmer suggested adding a drum solo to the trio's repertoire that Emerson began to weigh up the prospect of how the piece could be executed by ELP. Lake and Palmer were up for it but it required some thought when it came to designing an arrangement that would work with everyone's strengths in mind.

Emerson got in touch with Ginastera's publishers. In their response, they insisted that it would be unlikely that the composer would allow any of his works to be adapted. Despite this, they did advise Emerson that he should talk with Ginastera face to face. Consequently, Emerson flew to Geneva to talk to the composer. Upon playing the new arrangement to him, Emerson was granted the permission to proceed. Emerson recalled of the meeting; "He played our recording of 'Toccata' on a tape recorder. After a few bars he stopped the tape... and exclaimed 'Diabolic!' I thought he said 'diabolical' and expected him to show us the door. He had been listening to the tape in mono and our recording was in stereo. I jumped up and switched the machine to stereo hoping he would listen again. It transpired that he wasn't concerned about that at all. He listened again and declared 'Terrible!', which actually was a compliment. 'You've captured the essence of my music like no one else has before,' the great maestro said."

Both 'Karn Evil 9: 1st Impression' and 'Toccata' were used as part of the setlist for a series of concerts that took place across Europe beginning in late March 1973. It was around the same time that a new song was introduced to the repertoire: 'Still... You Turn Me On' was written by Lake. The semi-acoustic number brought a mellow balance to a set that was dominated by more abrasive numbers. Not only that, but as a romantic short song, it also got a fair amount of radio play, thus boosting the band's profile overall.

It wasn't always easy to get support from across all avenues of the media though. 'Jerusalem', an adaptation of Hubert Parry's hymn, with lyrics from the preface to William Blake's *Milton* poem, was banned by the BBC on the grounds of being in poor taste (the way in which the BBC had a reputation for trying to censor and dictate the nation's morals had earned it the nickname of Auntie; it had made a habit of being on the lookout — and keen to ban — content which it deemed too sexual or too overt in drug references).

"I can only assume that the motive for banning it would be that it was patriotic and that we were somehow blaspheming something cherished by the nation," said Lake. "We did it as well as we could and there was no mockery about it."

Around the period in which *Brain Salad Surgery* was made, there were some tracks recorded that would make their appearances on later albums; 'When The Apple Blossoms Bloom In The Windmills Of Your Mind I'll Be Your Valentine' and 'Tiger In A Spotlight'. Also, the title song of 'Brain Salad Surgery' wasn't included on the album itself. With the exception of his drum solo in 'Toccata', *Brain Salad Surgery* was the first ELP album where Palmer had no songwriting credits. Despite this, over the years, he has still said that the album is a favourite of his.

Brain Salad Surgery took nine months to complete. Lake considered, "It's certainly taken longer to write and put together than others, but after you've made four albums, people expect a certain thing from you and it's harder to come up with something that'll surprise them. A lot of bands go into solo ventures to avoid the monotony of playing the same style of music. Although we'll get into solo albums ourselves one day, the real answer for us is just to work harder and longer within the band. So when we do make solo albums, it won't be through frustration."

In comparison to the mood of *Trilogy* and *Tarkus*, *Brain Salad Surgery* sounds darker. Aware of this, Lake considered that the reason may have been on account of a number of factors, including how Eddy Offord, who had engineered ELP's previous albums, was absent (the role was given to Chris Kimsey and Jeff Young instead).

"Firstly, every engineer has a palette," said Lake. "And it's amazing how different a group can sound in different studios. Secondly, unlike the previous albums, *Brain Salad Surgery* is almost a live recording done in a studio. The sound was quite raw and quite ambient."

In October 1973, it wasn't long after the recording sessions had finished that the tracks for *Brain Salad Surgery* were mixed. It was released shortly after to reviews that were, in the main, positive. Negative ones like that which featured in *Rolling Stone* were arguably in the minority.

Rolling Stone reviewed *Brain Salad Surgery* in January 1974; "On stage, ELP usually overcome the shortcomings of their records — insufficient intensity and lack of worthy material — by working hard and busting their asses to play with incredible tightness (witness *Pictures At An Exhibition*). In the studio, their vision and grandiose schemes dilute

The ELP Story - *A Time and a Place*

the tightness, resulting in things like *Brain Salad Surgery*, on which their shortcomings outweigh undeniable moments of brilliance. The result: another sadly uneven album from a group with technical gifts equal to that of any British trio. Save for an occasional blast like 'Lucky Man' or 'Take A Pebble', songs have not been ELP's strong suite. When Lake is good as a writer, he's very good; when he's off, he has a tendency towards overblown lyrics. Hence, lines like 'Do you want to be the lover of another/undercover/you can even be the man in the moon', which drag the conceptually sound 'Still... You Turn Me On' to near-farcical proportions. And variation or not, each ELP disc has contained a needless nonsensical whimsy like this one's 'Benny The Bouncer' — each a terrible waste of the band's talent and the listener's time."

"Two shorter, instrumental-based pieces fare better. One, an adaptation of Albert Ginastera's Piano Concerto No.1, fourth movement, was rearranged by Keith Emerson with an eye towards the piece's inherent violence. The result so moved Mr G. that his unsolicited review is printed in the liner notes. Enough said. The other, an adaptation of the olde Englishe hymn 'Jerusalem', is pulled off with particular aplomb by Lake, whose interpretative vocals often take him beyond the limits of less impressive lyrics. The real meat of this platter, though, is the 'Karn Evil 9' suite whose three movements comprise roughly a side and a quarter of the disc. Another tour-de-force where ELP pull out all the sonic stops, this time around the themes of a tri-part epic battle between man and his surroundings. Emerson's keyboards whizz and speak, Lake and Carl Palmer hustle to keep perfect, imaginative time. Nonetheless, it's but a shell of its onstage self — where here they cook, in concert ELP's presentation of this number boils over and vaporises. This LP only convinces me that ELP really ought to record all their material in concert, for short of that I fear we're doomed to more albums like *Brain Salad Surgery* — another record that shows this fine band to mixed effect."

From *Billboard*: "The trio has gone ahead and created a complex, exciting sonic experience which touches on several bases — heady rock, flowing jazz and some zesty pop material. The softness of previous works has been replaced by a hard-driving, ethereal in places, kind of project. 'Still... You Turn Me On' incorporates Keith Emerson's happy time Barrelhouse piano and Carl Palmer's crisp brush work on snares. Greg Lake's vocals throughout blend vitally. '2nd Impression' is very jazz flavoured with a small trio sound built around fast 4/4 drumming and some fine piano playing. A Moog provides an eerie yet compelling sound on the other cuts."

From *Cash Box*: "Keith, Greg and Carl keep on proving that different is often better, especially on their latest bit of Manticore magic. The LP, a marvellous collection featuring some spectacular work on custom Moog synthesisers and Moog polyphonic ensemble by Emerson, and some devastating guitar and percussive artistry by Lake and Palmer, its strength is its grasp of subtly interwoven musical textures and feelings, highlighted by 'Jerusalem' and 'Karn Evil 9', an epic concept piece receiving four distinct impressions from the musicians. Truly a giant step for the trio, the package is a sure-fire bestseller."

From *Sounds*: "Now, I know a lot of people who don't really like ELP, but like this album... It seems to be their most uncluttered and melodic album to date, and certainly the rockiest. I would be very interested to know whether there's been any kind of musical exchange — both ways — between ELP and their new signing, the excellent Stray Dog. Having heard one or two cuts that didn't make this album, I would say that there has been, which is all for the good. 'Jerusalem' is rendered basically as per school hymn book with fine instrumental embroidery via Keith Emerson. 'Still... You Turn Me On', written and sung by Greg Lake, is a fine semi-acoustic song with neatly turned lyrics... 'Benny The Bouncer' is a straightforward beer and skittles foray. Emerson hammers away at the piano in frantic style, reminiscent of Humphrey Lyttelton's 'Bad Penny Blues', if you know it. 'Toccata' is Emerson's interpretation of Alberto Ginastera's Piano Concerto No.1, fourth movement. Side two and the remainder of side one is given over to the massive 'Karn Evil 9', a kind of future glimpse to a time when there's an eventual confrontation between man and the machines he has created, which are now imbued with their own independent existence. Apart from a couple of splendid drum solos from Palmer, Mr Emerson is to be heard trilling mightily like the old Nice days. There are some excellent lines too... I don't know whether consciously ELP have tried to bring about a change in their music, or whether it's me. Whatever. It has worked."

Writing for a local American newspaper, one journalist made an intelligent and well-considered point with regards to the album; "Time. That's important with *Brain Salad Surgery*. It's going to take quite a bit of time. Because while it's true the album is phenomenal in nearly every way — both technically and structurally — it's also perplexing. And difficult to deal with. And something that requires careful attention a number of times. And something that's worth every minute of time. Long-time ELP fans will find it somewhat more into rock 'n' roll sounds than the classic adventures the group has so often dabbled in in the past. Not screaming-loud English rock 'n' roll or anything, just not quite classically oriented. It's still terribly literate, the arrangements as intricate and complex as anything you're likely to hear and the overall sounds as diverse as anything on the market."

"The major cut on the album is a thing called 'Karn Evil 9', a piece taking up one third of side one and all of side two, and all a piece which Greg Lake describes as 'a very broad look at the evolution of man'. It's a work in three movements, of which the first offering is a retrospective view of the world as a person might see it two-thousand years or so from today. The general feeling of the movement is that the world today is a freak show. The second movement — or impression, as Lake calls them — is a transitional thing, more abstract, taking you from two-thousand years in the future all the way back to the beginning of things in caves. Sort of a history, commenting on man's mistakes. Not a protest, mind you, just a story. The last impression tells of a world governed by a computer where you load up your problems and the computer goes on to run the show. Not necessarily of moral terms, but always on pragmatic ones. The lyrics which tell you all of this are slightly cryptic, offered in half-finished thoughts, elaborate metaphors and vague statements about the state of things."

"The music which accompanies all of this is spacey but effective. Keith Emerson sets the mood (doesn't he always?) mainly with his custom-built Moog, his piano and his organ. Lake's bass (mainly bass, he does more) and Palmer's drums punctuate it with kinky rhythms while adding a strong sense of impending doom. It's one of those things which only ELP could pull off. And no, it's not pretentious at all. Complex and intricate, yes, but not pretentious. It would only be pretentious if all the complexity were of no purpose. But it does have a purpose — roughly to mirror the machine-like sick society which the lyrics depict — and is therefore functional. In a lighter vein — you need one after something like 'Karn Evil 9' — the album also offers 'Toccata', a sprightly and bouncy version of Ginastera's Piano Concerto No.1, fourth movement, performed mainly by Emerson and his synthesiser. 'Jerusalem', a traditional English hymn sped up and set to a non-traditional arrangement, 'Benny The Bouncer', a hymn to two 1950s teddy boys that rocks more than the rest of the album, and 'Still... You Turn Me On', a soft, easy thing to give your nerves a chance to unwind. It's a nice balance the choice of material achieves. After the overpowering 'Karn Evil 9', you can calm down and lighten up with one of the shorter cuts. In any case, the album's going to be a hard act for ELP to follow. It's that good."

****

Following the release of *Brain Salad Surgery*, and of course, rehearsals, ELP set off on a world tour from 14th November 1973 that continued until 21st August 1974.

In March 1973, it was reported in *New Musical Express*; "Shortly the band embark on a world tour, described as the 'biggest production spectacular ever mobilised', which will involve them playing inside a specially-constructed arch — a proscenium — complete with stage and curtains. The proscenium will be transported to every gig." To which Lake explained, "The real beauty of it for us, is that every night we're playing in the same box. Only the people in front will change. Also, from the point of view of a production, it's far more flexible. We can use the lights in the same position every night; we don't have to draw the curtains until we're exactly ready; altogether we can feel at home wherever we're playing… It'll help us and the audience reach higher peaks, which is basically what music is all about. We can get the audience to a greater level of excitement or bring them down for a more moody or tranquil thing. It'll help us stretch the extremes… I'm as sure as hell about it, because it adds something you can never get on a record. That special feeling of spontaneous elation you should ideally be able to get every night. Some people can do it almost every night — like James Brown — because he's spent years trying to achieve it. Maybe musically he's not doing anything that great, yet he can completely capture an audience. Also, as ELP, we have a lot of old numbers and songs that people expect to hear, and it's great to perform those old numbers with new visual trips — to perform those numbers with new things to heighten the effect… if a song's about water and you can lay a waterfall on people, that's nice, isn't it? It's a wonderful thing because it makes it all a bit more dreamlike, which to me is why people go to concerts anyway — to get away from things — to escape for a while."

Still though, as the journalist noted, "The disadvantages of the structure are, of course, blatantly obvious. It weighs twenty tons and takes fifty guys to move it. But Lake shrugs this off with 'it's not my problem' and obviously he and the band are prepared to overcome any obstacle, or pay people to overcome obstacles for them, simply to extend the effect of their concerts further."

In order to facilitate what would become the iconic theatrics of the band's live performances (Emerson's mid-air spinning piano and Palmer's revolving drum kit included), the group carried nearly forty tons of equipment, all of which took five hours to unpack and set up. It included a thirty-channel board discrete quadraphonic public address sound system (which had been provided by International Entertainers Service) and a state-of-the-art lighting system (designed by Judy Rasmussen) —

consisting of large ladders at each corner of the stage and two arches installed above the performance area.

A journalist writing for a local newspaper reported in November 1973; "It was men versus machines last night at the Miami Jai-Alai Fronton. Ultimately, the machines won out. Keith Emerson, Greg Lake and Carl Palmer treated an audience of five-thousand to one extravaganza of sight and sound — with the emphasis on sound. The occasion was the first night for the English group's first American tour in a-year-and-a-half. It coincides with the release of their fifth album, *Brain Salad Surgery*. That, naturally, was the starting point for the show. 'We're going to play some songs you're not familiar with,' keyboard artist Emerson told the audience. 'We're not either, so we'll learn together.' The triumvirate then proceeded into a concert of most unusual proportions in the rock world. Emerson, his long sandy hair cascading onto a black leather jacket shining with silver studs, jumped into the audience and walked up the centre aisle during a high point in 'Tarkus'. The audience ate it up."

"Other flashy notes to the show included projections on the stage wall of the group's three-letter symbol and photos of desolate land and stampeding wild horses. Palmer was applauded loudly midway through the show when his elevated drum stand began to revolve, revealing Chinese dragons painted in bright colours on the backs of two enormous gongs. And, as if that weren't enough of a visual treat, Emerson ended the group's set by turning his computer-like instrument to the audience. The flashing colours added to the effect of 'Karn Evil 9', about the world of computers. Soon, smoke began billowing from the machine's bottom, as wing-like projections began rising from the sides. Before the audience realised the smoke was not part of the well-programmed concert, the machine shorted out — putting an end to the amazement."

"But the group returned with an eventual encore — 'The Great Gates Of Kiev' from their *Pictures At An Exhibition* album. All in all, it was more than two hours of well-synthesised classical rock in the inimitable tradition of Emerson, Lake and Palmer. The only feature that marred the show was a constant buzz in the sound system. During more quiet numbers, when Emerson sat alone at the piano, the buzz was magnified one-hundred times. Hopefully, this will be corrected tonight when they play again at 8pm at the Fronton." (Was there really a technical fault or did the journalist perceive the special effects simply as such? The jury is certainly out on that one! Still though, it's all testament to the conviction with which ELP did their live shows).

Another journalist wrote of the same performance; "Opening night rarely comes to Miami, but Wednesday at the Jai-Alai Fronton, Emerson,

You Could Be Anything

Lake and Palmer kicked off their twenty-four-city US tour with a dazzling, ear-shattering performance of electronic rock 'n' roll. Despite some rough edges and occasional problems with their massive sound system, an evening of *Brain Salad Surgery* with Emerson, Lake and Palmer was every bit as unusual and bizarre as the name of their latest show implies. After beginning the programme with 'Jerusalem' and 'Toccata', two cuts from their new album, featuring Keith Emerson's screaming keyboard wizardry and Carl Palmer on synthesised drums, Emerson made a poignant observation that went a long way towards explaining the evening. 'Thank you and hello,' he said, stepping to the microphone, dressed in a black studded jacket and pants. 'We're not doing much to help the energy crisis we understand you have over here, but don't worry, we laid a cable under the Atlantic and we're getting our power direct'."

"Emerson's equipment alone comprised a double-tier Hammond organ (which he often played simultaneously), a synthesiser control board, a grand piano, electric piano, and amplified honky-tonk stand-up. Lording over that was Carl Palmer's pagoda of drums, kettle drums, gongs, chimes and cymbals, all contained on a wooden elevated structure that rotated in circles during one of his solos. Alternating between sections from *Brain Salad Surgery* and older hits such as 'Lucky Man' and 'Hoedown', their music touched on strains of everything from jazz to musical ragtime piano. And as is customary with all of Keith Emerson's performances since his early days with The Nice, there were also surprises. Notably, the oscilloscope that he wielded like a machine gun, creating a wall of screaming sounds as he raced amongst the audience. Also of note: the first performance of 'Karn Evil 9', an extended number from the latest album that incorporates all the divergent strains of the band, and may well become a definitive Emerson, Lake and Palmer classic."

On his approach to performing 'Karn Evil 9', Emerson told *Sounds* in December 1973; "It's important for me to put that point across of the difference between a machine playing the theme in relation to what we play and trying to drive the point across to the audience that it's computers and things which are making them redundant. And I purposely programmed the synthesiser to play the theme that we just played to make the effect more pronounced. We also wanted to counter, in a way, accusations in the past that ELP are "mechanical" in their music. I can base what I'm talking about on facts as, like when I left school, I worked on IBM equipment and I was going to learn to become a programmer for those things. But man, it was so boring. I purposely used to put faults in the machine to brighten up a dull day."

The following review, written in November 1973 for a local Tennessee-based newspaper under the heading of "Emerson, Lake, Palmer: Love It Or Hate It", is a fantastic example of how some audiences — including venue security — were not quite sure what to expect when it came to going to see ELP play live:

"Whatever the Emerson, Lake and Palmer concert was or was not Sunday night, it most certainly altered the audience's conception of music. Constant cascades of complex melodies rained upon the 7,340 listeners from four directions in an incomparable display of audible anarchy. If you happened to dig what was happening to your ears, you could lapse into musical heaven, entirely isolated from verbal communication originating anywhere but the stage. If you were among the unfortunate minority who dropped in on the wrong show, you faced a possible hearing loss and mental mangling by the spectacle beneath the spotlights. Beneath the battery of colourful lights, Keith Emerson had gone raving mad on his keyboard and the audience frequently seemed ready to fall on its knees in worship. Emerson was surrounded by two Moog synthesisers, two Hammond organs, one electric piano and one honky-tonk piano. The instruments were stacked nearly ten feet high on one side, and were covered in flashing coloured lights, viewing screens and more wires than a telephone switchboard. Emerson sometimes worked on two or more of the boards simultaneously, his hands barely reaching the keys. His frenzy increased until he was smashing one organ against the floor and finally pushed it over. In his tight black leather suit, the master of the keyboards became lord of the audience, satanically manipulating their response with each twitch of his fingers. Reinforcing the spell, he grabbed a small board and jumped to the auditorium floor to charm them individually."

"Although there were no weak moments — only superlative experiences — the concert was dominated by the melody of 'Karn Evil 9' from the group's *Brain Salad Surgery* album. Largely instrumental cuts from *Tarkus* also were particularly effective, as were sections from the group's recent *Trilogy* album. Percussionist Carl Palmer further added to the musical mystique by banging away at Chinese gongs and ringing a bell hanging overhead from an oriental arch. His most clever surprise was to rotate the drum platform to reveal in semi-darkness the figure of a dragon painted on the back of the gongs. However, the evening's biggest surprise came when two Metro policemen walked onto the stage in the middle of a song. One of them whispered something in guitarist Greg Lake's ear, bringing the show to a standstill and proliferating heated shouts from the audience. 'I'll tell you about what he told me and you can take it from there,' Lake told his fans. 'They're asking you to all sit down or they're going to pull the power off our instruments and turn on the house lights.'

Emerson toyed with his keyboard in an effort to distract the now angry crowd. Then the musicians left the stage as the lights were switched on."

"Backstage, a heated discussion followed, in which police officer J.W. Irvin told concert promoter Joe Sullivan, 'If we tell Chief Mott about this, there won't be any more of these concerts in here next year.' Mott was not available for comment yesterday. Irving later explained, 'We didn't want to interrupt. We told the people with the band several times to ask the kids to sit down and they played two more songs before we did anything.' Sullivan said, 'The police get a little overly anxious in situations like this. The kids weren't causing any problems. They were blocking the aisles and the band asked me to clear them before the show, which I did. However, the band has its show carefully worked out and can't always stop during a transition from one song to the next, so they were probably waiting for the right moment to have the audience sit down.' The band's tour manager, Alex King, said, 'We've handled crowds thirty-times as large as this. These kids were doing nothing but leaning on the barriers down front. There was no problem, no riot, and the show should not have been stopped.' Even with the interruption, a young man who attends most rock concerts in Nashville declared, 'This is the best concert I've ever been to.' In the seat behind, a girl covered her ears with her hands. 'This is entirely too loud,' she complained. Her date added, 'The prisoners in North Vietnam were never subjected to such suffering'."

RPM reported in December 1973; "Latest superstars to hit Toronto's Maple Leaf Gardens, Keith Emerson, Greg Lake and Carl Palmer, also stole the award for best concert of the year — and by quite a margin. It's also surprising that the Gardens is still standing without being blown out of its foundation. Keith Emerson, in association with Greg Lake and Carl Palmer, comprise one of, if not *the*, most powerful triumvirate known to contemporary space-age rock... Out of the blackness, with only electricity humming and indicator lights flashing, the show was born. ELP were ready to perform some *Brain Salad Surgery* on the unsuspecting crowd and from anaesthetic to post-surgery relaxation, it was a successful operation. There was not too much familiarity with the general concept of the album, since the only exposure fans got was through the airwaves and even then the dose was minimal. So it was up to the band to outline what was happening and leave the rest up to our imagination. Those three human beings up there on stage had control of the building and its 15,000-odd inhabitants. The massive mixing station plopped in the centre of the floor, the extravagant lighting works that criss-crossed beams to bathe the stage with gaseous colour, and the incredible 360-degree quad sound system were enough to get you high without exterior help."

"Emerson was surrounded by keyboards, keyboards and more keyboards, all fed through his enormous computer-like synthesiser, and like a mad scientist preparing for a spaceship lift off, he fiddled and dialled and adjusted and engineered sounds that were only common to the age of 2001. And when the quad sound clicked in, it was over for most of our minds. The music he played and sounds he generated, were indescribable and it is unlikely that anyone out of the audience had ever experienced anything resembling it. Nonetheless, it was not hard to realise that this was only one third of a whole. Greg Lake takes charge of the vocals, and his voice, reminiscent of the early Crimson days, has electrostatic clarity to it. He switches from bass guitar (which gives him that watery sound familiar to ELP) to six-string acoustic and back throughout the whole set. It was his solo rendition of 'Lucky Man', a classic smash, that melted the audience with appreciation. To complete the whole was Carl Palmer's elaborate percussion area, soon to be recognised as foremost in his field. As well as the others, Palmer treated the audience to his own brand of drum solo, revolving on a pod and climaxing with strobe lights flashing in total darkness. It was surely not your ordinary drum solo. His instruments were also fed through the synthesiser and proved to have great effect, blasting out of the four speaker systems. He has developed his musical area to the point where whatever is next is in the unimaginable category. But then that is true about ELP's whole trip!"

"It is at this point that I'd like to take some time to describe a unique characteristic of concerts of today: pre-concert and intermission activities. It all began with one giant beach ball being tossed around the crowd. Now, the activities have matured to whipping frisbees, toilet paper rolls, and believe it or don't, inflatable dummies (and female ones at that). It turns out to be excellent recreation, ideal and unique of giant rock concerts of our time. Those fireballs that get tossed around are also a lot of fun. Apart from *Brain Salad*, the band got into some 'Tarkus' action and 'Take A Pebble', from their first album. But it wasn't until Emerson flicked his machine into high gear that everyone's mind blew. He managed to circulate the sound from speaker system to speaker system, ever increasing in frequency and in effect, immersing the Gardens in an electronic storm of modern music technology only to freak the crowd out with a magnesium explosion and a farewell. Fifteen minutes of standing ovation, the likes of which was uncommonly strong, bought the group back for about twenty minutes of more surgery. And then it was over. And as in past super concerts, all that was left was a sigh."

Regarding how the tour had been worked out in great detail, Emerson told *Sounds* in December 1973; "It has to be. The lighting has to be pretty well together, mainly because they can't improvise. There were just a few minor changes that had to be made at the beginning of the tour. Like originally, the piece with the Moog at the end finished with it panning the theme from the third movement of 'Karn Evil 9' and we left the stage, but people didn't understand it. We needed some sort of finality to the set, to make the point... The stage ending doesn't take away from the meaning of the piece, but it was very necessary to do this for the live performance: on the actual recording, it was left as an unanswered question, because obviously with the subject we're handling, there is no answer... Another thing was that one of the numbers had to be transposed down a tone or so because Greg got laryngitis or broke his vocal cords trying to sing the number. I still like the improvisation parts — they differ from night to night."

In January 1974, *Billboard* reported on a Madison Square Garden performance; "Emerson, Lake and Palmer demonstrated why they are considered one of the world's premier rock groups last week with their two dazzling performances at Madison Square Garden. The group mounted a two-pronged attack, combining musical virtuosity with spellbinding visuals that culminated in their encore of Mussorgsky's *Pictures At An Exhibition*. Toward the end of the piece, the group broke out in a version of 'Silent Night' with Greg Lake joined by a sixty-voice choir. As snow began falling on the singers and the group from inside the Garden, Keith Emerson shattered the calm with a frantic assault on his organ, sending it toppling across the stage. From the opening number, a spicy version of Aaron Copland's 'Hoedown', the Manticore act had the audience enthralled. Most of the attention is focused on Emerson and his arsenal of synthesisers, organs and pianos, which he handles with formidable skill, often playing two or three keyboards at the same time, transmitting swirling patterns of sound around the Garden through the group's quadraphonic PA system. The group performed material from the latest album, *Brain Salad Surgery*, but received a more ecstatic response to older favourites like 'Tarkus', 'Take A Pebble', and 'Lucky Man', featuring Lake on vocals and acoustic guitar. Carl Palmer's drumming and percussion work now includes an array of gongs, chimes and bells. The evening's only problems came with Greg Lake's vocals, which here lacked clarity despite his impressive range."

Cash Box also enthused; "On the last leg of their American tour, Keith Emerson, Greg Lake and Carl Palmer presented one of the best shows I've seen in a long, long time. With a stage full of equipment including two gongs, a two-hundred-year-old church bell, and approximately thirteen keyboard instruments, the trio opened their set with an outstanding version of 'Jerusalem'... The sound system was placed all around the Garden and provided the best sound ever heard there; it was simply perfect. We patrons should tip our hats to the sound mixer for his efforts. Greg's vocals, especially on 'Take A Pebble' and 'Lucky Man', were crystal-clear throughout the evening. During the course of the Monday show, the second coming on Tuesday, the crowds sat in amazement as they watched the group recreate many favourite pieces with all the theatrics added."

"Some of these same showbiz grabbers have been phased out, such as Emerson placing knives in his Hammond organ, but great new ones have taken their place. During one of the selections which featured Carl Palmer and his synthesised drum kit, all of a sudden his whole kit starts to revolve as he keeps going at it. Keith Emerson has a piano at the side of the stage, to which he strapped himself in, began playing, and both of them rise up off the floor, and then started going around. I don't know whether one can visualise Emerson playing piano upside down, but he did. This happened several times and he looked like he was having a great time. He also had his synthesisers flashing lights and then going up in smoke. The new album was performed in its entirety with a screen suspended from the ceiling showing various pictures and images. The group's music speaks for itself. And these extra added attractions were just that; sure, they can be eliminated, but they are great as they are, so why not have them. The Garden looked beautiful as everyone lit matches calling for an encore. The encore incorporated Lake singing 'Silent Night' with a large choir behind him and snow falling from the ceiling. It was simply beautiful. An outstanding evening it was, from Emerson, Lake and Palmer."

"At Madison Square we went on and we did those things with the choir and a whole bunch of other sections without rehearsing them," Emerson admitted to *Sounds* in December 1973.

On 2nd February 1974, in the main arena at the Anaheim Convention Centre in California, ELP's performance was recorded. It was released as a three-disc anthology — *Welcome Back My Friends To The Show That Never Ends — Ladies And Gentlemen* — later that year. An amount of the same material was broadcast on the *King Biscuit Flower Hour*. The live album got to number six in the UK chart and to number four on the Billboard 200. It was the highest US chart position ever achieved by ELP.

In December 1974, *Record World* considered that *Welcome Back My Friends To The Show That Never Ends* "will certainly be a priority item during the Christmas sales season" and that "considered the progenitors of classical rock, the sterling British trio has successfully managed to transfer all the excitement of a live show to their records".

Also; "The growth in their expertise and finesse is demonstrated by beguiling and startling renditions of 'Tarkus', 'Take A Pebble' and the showstopper 'Karn Evil 9', which is given an expensive treatment. Keith Emerson's impressive piano technique coupled with Carl Palmer's ambitious percussive interludes and Greg Lake's outstanding vocals and fine bass renditions are the major headliners. The overall effect is one that guarantees sustained listening enjoyment. In live concerts, few groups can match the power of ELP. With platinum discs awarded for *Emerson, Lake and Palmer*, *Trilogy*, *Tarkus*, *Pictures At An Exhibition* and *Brain Salad Surgery*, these three musicians have established pre-eminent positions on the contemporary music scene. Even more enticing are the plans for the future, which include the release of three very unique and individual solo albums for each member — currently in the formative stages — and another possible US and European tour. Emerson, Lake and Palmer will continue to record for Atlantic Records under the Manticore label. The ongoing association has been a very productive one and should continue to be so with their upcoming new release."

It was on 6th April 1974, when ELP co-headlined with Deep Purple at the California Jam Festival. Held at the Ontario Motor Speedway, there were 350,000 paying fans in attendance. ELP's performance was broadcast by the ABC television network — it was they who sponsored the festival. The audio recording of the performance first appeared officially on the 1998 album, *Then And Now*.

A local American paper had considered in December 1973; "It's taken over three years for Emerson, Lake and Palmer to convert their potential as splendid English musicians into a classical rock sound which makes them answer to no one. But doing it they are — with a flair for turning the usual into the unusual. That's a polite way of saying the group plays a brand of cosmic electronic music that either turns you on or leaves you flat. Seldom is there any in between. In any event, they're so awesome at what they do that they can't be ignored. ELP is perhaps the latest manifestation of a rock phenomenon particular to England's most brilliant contemporary bands. That is, their music gradually attains an infectious popularity in North America after having appealed for a long time to a select core of rock audiences, as witnessed in the past with Pink Floyd, The Moody Blues, Jethro Tull and Humble Pie. Indicative of ELP's bulging popularity is their desire to perform at festivals, which they've avoided in the past."

To which Lake explained; "Festivals have always been something we avoided because they're seldom organised. But next year, the band will do more festivals because we've reached a stature where we can dictate the structure of a festival."

At the time, the California Jam set records for the loudest amplification system ever installed, the highest paid attendance, and highest gross. The event has gone down in history for a number of reasons, both economic and entertaining.

Deep Purple was given the choice of when they would go on stage to perform. Their guitarist, Ritchie Blackmore, was particularly explicit about the fact that he wanted to be on stage after sunset. Such decision resulted in ELP being scheduled for the last performance. Deep Purple's performance at the California Jam was one of their first with their third line-up of David Coverdale on vocals and Glenn Hughes on bass and additional vocals.

When it was time for Deep Purple to perform their set, sunset had not yet arrived. As a result, Blackmore locked himself in his trailer in protest. Eventually, after much to-ing and fro-ing, Deep Purple finally graced the stage just as it was starting to get dark but as fans were about to witness, Blackmore wasn't happy by this point. The result was a TV camera being obliterated as he furiously jabbed his guitar into it.

Not ones to have their thunder be stolen, ELP's set featured memorable theatrics that included extended synthesiser frenzies and a Hammond organ being played from the wrong end. It was so much more than that though. Emerson had opted to float in the air on a piano — not only that, but he threw in a number of somersaults too. The stunt was everything that an ELP fan could hope for and more. A sight to behold, caught on tape and in front of an immensely large audience. Fantastic!

Keith explained how the stunt came to be; "I think having a pilot's licence helped a little bit. One of my road crew said, 'We found this guy that used to work in the circus and he does a lot of things for TV and special effects, and he's made something that might interest you, it's a piano that spins round', and I immediately responded, 'Oh, that sounds interesting'. I happened to be within the New York area and I was driven over to Long Island to a guy called Bob McCarthy, and there in the background, he had this piano situated. So he called his wife down from upstairs and said, 'Darling could you demonstrate this for Keith?'. I looked on, I wasn't quite sure what to expect. His wife comes down and sits on the seat and up she goes in the air and proceeds to spin around. I thought, 'Well that's great!'. Then Bob asked me, 'Do you want to have a go at it?'... 'Yeah, okay'. You need to understand, below the keyboard there's an inverted-tee, like a bar. You wrap your legs around the down pipe and put your heels under the inverted-tee. Then you go up in the air and try and do your best to play. It was a little difficult to play at first because of the centrifugal force, so it wasn't easy. I think we actually used it for the first time at Madison Square Garden, it was a Christmas concert. People in the audience were so astounded they couldn't quite believe what they were seeing. Later on that coming year, the California Jam came up and I said we have to do that there. Bob drove the whole contraption down to the California Jam and there was very little space to set it up. There were loads of bands up on that stage, all having to do their set and then getting their equipment off. Now, with the Moog, the Hammonds, Carl's gongs and everything, it was hard enough to just get that on stage. We had the spinning piano and everything that went along with it and we tried to find a place to situate it. It ended up going just at the end of the stage, so when the piano went up it was literally over the heads of the audience. After that, with every TV show I did came the question, 'Keith, how do you spin around on that piano?'. I'd say, 'What about my music?'. When I had the honour of meeting the great jazz pianist Dave Brubeck just before he died, he said, 'Keith, you've got to tell me how do you spin around on that piano?'. Dave Brubeck was ninety years old then and I said, 'Dave, don't try it!'."

Years later, Lake explained, "It was a Steinway piano. The idea was that Keith would sit in it — he would be strapped in. There would be a lot of smoke, and the piano would start to rise up into the air. It would get about fifteen, twenty feet in the air, and then it would start to spin. With him on it!"

Injuries and the ergonomic demands of the stunt were such that sadly, it came with a shelf life. Lake added, "He'd be playing while all of this was going on. You had this spinning piano, and there would be more smoke and more smoke until the piano was spinning in smoke — and then there'd be a huge explosion, and it would disappear. Now, I can't tell you how it was made to disappear. But that's what happened... There were a few times that Keith actually hurt himself doing it. So, we had to stop it. But for a while it was very impressive."

In the main, apart from where some journalists commented on minor technical faults and/or where the music simply wasn't to their own taste, reviews for the whole of the tour supporting *Brain Salad Surgery* were positive. As one journalist said in August 1974 of a performance that took place at the Hara Arena; "Fantastic, incredible, astounding, wonderful, beautiful, and exciting — they are all appropriate in describing Wednesday night's Emerson, Lake and Palmer concert... ELP played flawlessly for two solid hours." The journalist also noted that "the roar that greeted their first appearance on stage was deafening" and that the audience was "spellbound and applauding like lunatics as ELP thanked the crowd and left".

ELP's identity as a British band was such that even though they were big in America by this point, they didn't wish to change their sound.

"Fundamentally, you've got to go back to the roots of our music," said Lake. "Most American rock bands are based on a blues heritage. We're based on a European heritage, which stems ultimately from classical music. And classical music is much more complex than blues. But playing simple music well is as hard as playing complex music well. American bands have a looser attitude with what they write and play. With them, it's like jamming much of the time — that's what everybody does here in America. We could jam with the Grateful Dead, for instance, but it would be impossible for them to play with us."

However, ELP certainly didn't avoid improvisation. "It is important to go through a section of improvisation and play just what you feel like playing," said Emerson. "A lot of our music is very controlled and arranged and we just have to let ourselves go at certain points."

Indeed, the band were certain of their overall performance style and musical identity by that point. Lake said in March 1974; "It's true that classical musicians have turned off to a majority of rock music. And they have good reason to. Most rock music isn't very good, but that can be said of other types of music too. If classical music had been written to be played by electronic instruments, it would be no big deal for us to perform it. But we justify doing it by putting so much of ourselves and our own style of music into it."

"These theatrics are a very important part of our act," said Palmer. "But we're careful never to let them supersede the music. Most American musicians are still playing in t-shirts and jeans. When they come on stage, they look like part of the road crew. We dress up a little to try to project an image. I think the fans want to see you looking nice."

Towards the end of 1974, ELP decided that it was time for a break. It comes across that the band had been happy to put in the hours (and then some!) during the tour that had brought them so much success, but all the same, with hindsight, it is understandable as to how a feeling of burnout may have come about. "It's going to take me some time to relax," Emerson told *Sounds* in December 1973. "I could play another concert tonight. I don't feel as if I've just worked six weeks."

The band had made some bold decisions, which, based on their success by that point, had paid off. "We've experimented an awful lot, and tried various things, some of which have worked and some haven't," Emerson said. "A lot of bands around at the moment, I would consider "safe" bands. But we've done an awful lot and risked a lot of things, like on the European tour with that proscenium and lugging around seventy roadies."

Lake took the opportunity to catch up with family life and to travel.

He continued to write and release music though. By this time, ELP were tax exiles relocated to Switzerland, France, Canada and The Bahamas. It meant that they were restricted to only two months' stay in England per year. The extended break was certainly needed; by that point, ELP had been recording and touring every year since their formation in 1970. Emerson said that at this stage in their career, their musical direction had been "milked dry". Everyone agreed that time out was needed in order to consider what direction to go in next.

Even during the successful tour of 1973-74, each member of the band had been preparing solo work. Lake said in 1974; "We've all done a little bit on our solo albums... It comes in spurts in between all the other work. You can't really settle down to a long period on it, just bits and pieces, but it's coming." When asked about his opinion on solo albums, he added; "I think it stemmed from the players in bands who perhaps saw the day when their band broke up and whatever. It's an insecure life and I suppose they thought that to make a solo album would enhance their own identity. And so everybody was making solo albums, which kind of put me off a bit, and still does. I really don't want to make it come out like a solo album. It certainly won't be recorded like "The Great Lake Album". I want it to have a title and be an album in its own right. Then if people find out later that I've done it, then great and that would be a fantastic dream for me. But I want it to survive on its merits, and the main motive is to see what, without compromise, my music will bring forth. Because in a band, you compromise and happily so. But it's interesting to see what will happen when it's just me."

When asked if his solo album would be an acoustic one, Lake explained; "I suppose it's more me than anything. But I've always played in tough music bands all my life, The Gods and people like that, and really, it's part of me. In fact, on ELP albums, I usually put only one track down that's like an acoustic thing. I think anyway, I'm known for acoustic things for my solo spots. Peter Sinfield writes the lyrics and they are better than my own lyrics to my melodies. It's just like a flash of magic. It's a good combination that has worked for years. It worked in King Crimson and we've done some on *Brain Salad*. Of all the musicians, he's the one closest to me. He's the only one I could write lyrics with, and he writes exactly the lyrics that I want."

Chris Welch considered in 1974; "Greg's own music veers more towards the pretty ballad and meaningful song, usually written in collaboration with poet Peter Sinfield, and it is a cause for regret that perhaps more of this kind of material has not been forthcoming in ELP. But they are the kind of band with so much to play and choose from, where not everything can be made to fit. When there is a keyboard player like Keith Emerson around and a percussionist of the stature of Carl Palmer, then it's small wonder that Greg sometimes gets a mite overshadowed. But Lake's contributions should not be minimised. He plays a singularly attractive brand of acoustic guitar, while his vocal style often reminds me of a schooled John Lennon, the notes pitched spot-on but given just a shade of the nasal, cutting edge, to original ballads like 'C'est La Vie'."

It was in 1975 and whilst still officially a member of ELP that Lake had a hit single with 'I Believe In Father Christmas'. Lake said of writing the song, "I wrote it in my house in west London. I'd tuned the bottom string on my guitar from E down to D and got this cascading riff that you hear on the record." Co-writer Sinfield said, "Some of it was based on an actual thing in my life when I was eight years old, and came downstairs to see this wonderful Christmas tree that my mother had done. I was that little boy. Then it goes from there into a wider thing about how people are brainwashed into stuff. Then I thought, 'This is getting a bit depressing. I'd better have a hopeful, cheerful verse at the end.' That's the bit where me and Greg would've sat together and done it. And then I twisted the whole thing with the last line, 'The Christmas you get, you deserve', which was a play on 'The government you get, you deserve'. I didn't necessarily explain all the politics or the thoughts behind it. It's not anti-religious. It's a humanist thing, I suppose. It's not an atheist Christmas song, as some have said."

'I Believe In Father Christmas' got to number two in the UK and has been a seasonal staple ever since. Upon its release, the single sold at least 13,000 copies over just two days. Queen's 'Bohemian Rhapsody' claimed the number one spot that year. Lake said, "I got beaten by one of the greatest records ever made. I would've been pissed off if I'd been beaten by Cliff."

In 1976, Emerson released the single, 'Honky Tonk Train Blues'. With 'Barrelhouse Shake-Down' on the B-side, it got to number twenty-one in the UK. The lead track was written by Meade Lux Lewis, who had first recorded it in 1927.

Having struck up a rapport with a jazz trio by the name of Back Door when touring, Palmer produced their fourth album that was released in 1976, *Activate*. Saxophonist Ron Aspery and bassist Colin Hodgkinson co-wrote the song 'Bullfrog' with Palmer. It would go on to feature on *Works Volume 2*.

6.
Everything You've Ever Dreamed

Back from a break and refreshed for new innovations, in 1976, ELP began working on what would be their fifth studio album. Stewart Young recalled; "At that time there was a very savage tax structure in the country, so the lawyers advised us that we should record it outside the UK. We'd always had a good time in Switzerland, and we met a guy called Claude Nobs who used to run the Montreux jazz festival. He told us about this great studio in Montreux — it was a bit dramatic, but we all moved down and recorded there."

"We were at Mountain Studios for some time, about six months," Palmer recalled.

"It was fantastic," said Lake. "It was actually built beneath the casino in Montreux. It was just one of the top studios of the time. You'd book the studio out — twenty-four hours a day — and so it was a kind of living environment. But things did start to become undisciplined. When you record in a city, and you book a session, you turn up, you do it and then go home. When you're in a residential setting situation, you start coming and going at odd times. The discipline breaks down... We all rented houses, up and around Montreux. I had one right at the top of a mountain, right by the top of the clouds, which was actually very weird. And, you know, Switzerland is quite a strange place really — everything is just surreal."

ELP released *Works Volume 1* in March 1977. It is a double album where each member of the trio had one side of an LP for solo music, with the fourth side reserved for a collective effort.

The *Works* albums were released on the basis that each member wanted to shine in his own right, potentially even on solo albums. However, the marketing concept of putting it all on an album under the

ELP umbrella made the most sense. Lake said in 1978; "We obviously want to keep Emerson, Lake and Palmer together. Everybody in the group wants to establish his own identity. That's a fact of life."

"*Works* was the only way to keep the band together," said Emerson at the time. "Each of us originally started by doing solos."

"At one stage, Keith was thinking about doing a solo album of a piano concerto," Young recalled. "We came up with a compromise, so the concerto eventually ended up on the album. Because everybody obviously wanted the group to stay as a group, but there was a difference of opinion as to the best way to do that."

On balance, each member of ELP had already shown the propensity to be able to work successfully away from the band and by this point in their respective careers, each of them had an abundance of ideas within their own creative pallets. In 1977, Emerson explained how he went about choosing the sounds to use on each song; "Usually if I'm arranging a new piece of music, I don't want to use any of those sounds which I know about already. If I've got the sound in my head, I go 'Ah yes, I know how to go about that' — I'm wired up. I could do it that way, but usually what I tend to do is, from time to time, in my experimenting, I come across a thing quite by accident. I go, 'That's fantastic', and I jot that down. Usually at that time when I hear that particular sound I say, 'Well, I know what that's going to be used for'."

With lyrical assistance from Sinfield, Lake wrote five songs. He specifically wanted to avoid doing "just ballads" in favour of embracing a wider range of musical styles. As part of this, he incorporated orchestral overdubs to the songs. One of his songs, 'C'est La Vie', was released as a single. Sadly though, Lake called the album the "beginning of the end" of ELP on the basis that on future albums, he was no longer the producer. He also felt that despite their best efforts, *Works Volume 1* was not a "really innovative record".

That's not to say that morale was at an all-time low for the band though — far from it, in fact. "We really got on," Palmer recalled. "I mean, the band has always been three individuals just like it says in the name: Emerson, Lake and Palmer. When we played music together, it was the best time of our lives and probably for all of us it was the greatest time we ever had, when we actually got together and played. It was kind of everything outside of that, really [that was a problem] — we just weren't as compatible as people might have thought we were."

Besides, "*Works* was more complex than we projected it to be," Palmer said at the time. "It's basically for ourselves. We didn't expect the public to take to it too instantly. It's not a commercial album."

Everything You've Ever Dreamed

Vitally, when promoting *Works*, Lake provided some fascinating insight into his inspirations and thought process. He said of 'Hallowed Be Thy Name'; "It's a protest song. And as such, I suppose it's a bit corny. There was an age when there was a lot of protest songs. I just can't help it. There are things that go on these days I feel the same way about as I did ten years ago. They peeve me something. Certainly, they come out in my writing. Artists are sensitive people. I'm sensitive. I don't presume really to know anything. But I mean, I just understand more atoms of things, and I string them together and it makes a song. Really rather than communicating a message, it's a question of communicating a feeling. And I think what music's done in the last ten/fifteen years is raise the feeling and the spirit of people and help them to grow through their young life."

Carl Palmer's contribution to the album was also musically diverse. He confirmed, "My stuff on *Works* was quite eclectic, I must confess. I'm still like that, if you came to my house and looked through my record collection. It's pretty weird, if I'm honest. It's hard to listen to one genre of music for too long. Last night I was listening to Buddy Guy, a new album of his called *Sweet Tea*, and I've never been a Buddy Guy fan but I heard one track and it was just fantastic. It's just whatever gets me at the time. I've always listened to all kinds of different music."

The drummer's reworking of Prokofiev's *Scythian Suite* is impressive. Even with ELP's other classical adaptations in mind, the latter was a bold and charismatic contribution from the then twenty-six-year-old in the form of 'The Enemy God Dances With The Black Spirits'. Palmer recalled that he had not heard the original piece before; "But I had a friend who suggested it, saying, 'If you want something with a lot of bumping and grinding in it, it would definitely transfer to a contemporary kind of band...' That was it. I heard it and loved it, so we recorded it, without Keith knowing about it, and then I played it to him and of course he loved it too... It used to go down incredibly well. It's an extremely tough piece of music."

Works Volume 1 got to number nine in the UK and to number twelve on the US Billboard 200 chart — an impressive achievement, considering all the other genres of music that were rising in popularity at the time. In particular, ELP were aware of Britain's love for punk music. They certainly weren't intimidated by it though. Lake made his feelings on the genre clear: "I don't take any interest in the music. I saw it go up and I'll see it go down."

The track, 'Fanfare For The Common Man', was Emerson's adaptation of the 1942 composition by Aaron Copland. ELP released their version as a single in May 1977. It went to number two in the UK to become ELP's highest charting single there.

Emerson explained some of the changes he made to Copland's original piece; "It needed transposing, so I did that first. I wanted to improvise in a key that was sort of bluesy. It ended up in E. The rest of it was straightforward, really. In order to get the shuffle sound, the timing had to be changed, but it was common sense."

Lake said; "It was just wonderful how it came about: We were recording in Montreux, Switzerland, in 1976, and Keith was playing it as a piece of classical music. I played this shuffle bass line behind him and all of a sudden it started to connect. Then Carl came in and we three started to play it. Luckily, the engineer had a two-track running, and that is what's on the record — the first time we played through the piece."

Stewart Young recalled, "We had to get the permission of Aaron Copland, the composer. The publishing house said forget it. So I got Mr Copland's home number, called him up and he was very friendly on the phone. And he says 'Send it to me, let me listen'. And he loved it. He called me and said, 'This is brilliant, this is fantastic. This is doing something to my music'."

"Had he not liked it, I think we probably wouldn't have released it," said Lake. "We wouldn't have wanted to cause offence, I don't think. But he really liked the fact that at the end of it, we broke out into this improvisation; it was something that his music had inspired, it wasn't just a reproduction of his notes. I think he found a joy in that."

ELP's song had actually been recorded on a single microphone during that iconic jam session. Attempts were made to do other takes at a later date. "We tried to reproduce it again," said Palmer. "But we never quite got the excitement. I think it was the freshness of getting back together. So we bounced the quarter-inch over to the two-inch multi-track and then started overdubbing it from there. We decided to dub keyboards on top of the multi-track as it was bounced over, and then we dubbed on that bit of extra bass, some cymbals and stuff like that. The microphone was hanging in the middle of the room, so it captured everyone. So the version that was a hit, actually started off as a live demo."

"We felt that it would benefit from the original trumpet fanfare at the beginning," said Lake. "So we put that on, but I think everything else was pretty much as it was. I'm sure the actual body of the record is as it was recorded live."

"I think it may have been Ahmet Ertegun who suggested 'Fanfare For The Common Man' should be a single," Lake recalled. "I never liked the edited version, though. I always feel it's like, imagine if you had an oil painting and you cut away the corner, it wouldn't look so good. But radio play insists on a certain time, and you must conform or your record doesn't get played."

On recording the video for 'Fanfare For The Common Man', Lake recalled; "We had just heard that they wanted to release it as a single. My initial reaction was like, 'Well, no, we're too busy doing the rehearsals with the orchestra'. And I went up to the stadium and I was looking at this absolutely mind-blowing site, covered in virgin snow, with the Olympic rings lit up in neon lights at both ends. It was an eerie sight, begging for something to happen, and I thought, *video*! We got the crew to move the gear up to the stadium the next day to start recording. Of course, what we didn't plan was for it to be way below zero. My fingers would literally slip through the strings. So we had to record it in fairly short bursts, but it was a lovely film in the end."

"It was something like twenty degrees below, it was extremely cold," Palmer recalled. "We managed to shoot three times — a few cameras on one person, a whole take, the same on the next guy, the same on the next guy — and then one take of all of us playing together. But it was very, very cold. The music has lasted though. It has endured and it's been truly fantastic. Quality always lasts, and I sincerely believe that we had a lot of quality going there — we weren't just a prog band, we had pretty songs as well. So it was quite eclectic."

The last track on *Works Volume 1* is 'Pirates' — a prog epic that Lake admitted wasn't without its challenges technically, but certainly something that made for an incredible performance when played live. Palmer considered with hindsight, "'Pirates' was the last of the big ones. It's a terrific piece of music. Pete Sinfield, who was absolutely exceptional, came up with the idea, the whole concept, and I thought it all married up exceptionally well. It was recorded in Switzerland, Montreux, in Mountain Studios right on Lake Lucerne. I can't remember much of the recording, but it was all analogue so it was done in segments and there was probably a lot of editing. We could never play that stuff straight off. If you look at the master tape for *Tarkus*, for instance, it's got seventeen edits on it, all cut with a razorblade."

Additional material that was recorded in 1976, in addition to songs from previous studio sessions, was released as *Works Volume 2* in November 1977.

A local British newspaper considered of *Works Volume 1*; "ELP are fighting for their crown back after more than two-and-a-half years of recording silence. The double set contains a solo side by each member. And the fourth side boasts composite renderings from all three. Keith Emerson leads off with 'Piano Concerto No.1' with the London Philharmonic Orchestra. It's a shame the track doesn't sound as impressive as the title. Emerson plays dated numbers that lack depth or feeling, which are held together only by a sense of frustration. Greg Lake takes over side two with five love songs that sound pleasant enough. And by way of inspiration, 'Hallowed Be Thy Name' is the most laudable and worthwhile project on the entire album. Carl Palmer is the best of the bunch and side four is a cluttered, undemanding exercise that fades away with each revolution."

Another local British newspaper considered of the album; "Well here it is — the first record produce in a long, long time from the mighty ELP. And their ever-loving ever-patient legions of fans are certain to be more than delighted with the two-album set. Quite frankly, I've never been able to understand the overwhelming popularity of ELP. Apart from their lofty attitudes towards performing and recording, their music, while technically superb, has little to do with the excitement, feeling and spontaneity at the heart of our most major bands. This collection is a vehicle for excessive self-indulgence by the three individual members, each taking a side to pursue his own projects and coming together only on side four. Keith Emerson's contribution takes the form of 'Piano Concerto No.1', highly classical and divided into three movements. It's okay if you like that sort of thing, but tedious otherwise. The most accessible section of the album comes from Greg Lake, his set a predictable bunch of gentle songs written by himself and Pete Sinfield. Carl Palmer, for his part, has thrown in a curious hotch-potch of ideas that sound somehow unfinished, while side four, comprising of 'Fanfare For The Common Man' and 'Pirates' introduces for the first time the well-known distinctive sound of the band playing together. Personally, this is not an album I'd buy, but each one to his own — and there are going to be many thousands of people making this their own."

The reviewer's honesty is commendable; they have been honest about the fact that they have never really been that into ELP so of course, that colours their assessment of ELP's 1977 album. On balance though, the reviewer went to great lengths to express the fact that as a group, ELP sounded very divided on the album, purely owing to the nature of how it had been structured with regards to track listings.

Works Volume 1 was reviewed in *The Stage*; "A double album, which could have been a monstrous ego trip but fortunately isn't, in that it shows the very real talents of three diversified musicians who are, to a certain extent, victims of their overblown, over-theatrical approach to rock. Only side four has them all together on this occasion, featuring Copland's 'Fanfare For The Common Man'. Emerson's 'Piano Concerto No.1', which he plays with the London Philharmonic Orchestra conducted by John Mayer, proves that Emerson is a dexterous concert pianist but his composition is a curious ragbag of styles, predominantly late-nineteenth-century romantic but with a dedicated Stravinsky influence, and little in the way of thematic development. Greg Lake's side consists of rather characterless love songs, while Carl Palmer's contribution shows that at heart he is a big band drummer in the Buddy Rich mould."

Regarding the variety of moods and styles on his concerto, Emerson had his reasons. As he told *Rolling Stone* in 1977; "I wrote the first two movements of my concerto in a pleasant, pastoral style. Then my house in the English countryside burned down, and the final movement became more 'fuck you'. Aggressive."

Under the heading of "Magic Of ELP Returned After A Few Plays", one journalist wrote for a local British newspaper; "Since their formation, Emerson, Lake and Palmer have been one of the truly world-class rock bands. Their second album, *Tarkus*, set the rock world alight and over the past few years, they followed up with some superb work to place them right at the top of the tree. ELP have legions of fans in every country, who snap up every work as soon as it is released. The same happened with their last double album, *Works*, and no doubt the process will be repeated with their latest offering, *Works Volume 2*. But I wonder if this latest offering will be as well-liked as earlier albums?"

"When I first played *Works Volume 2*, I was shocked. It sounded nothing like the ELP I know and love. In fact, I did not return to the album for about a week, but after a few plays, the old magic came to my notice. Right away, I must say, this album is not as good as earlier albums. But for the true ELP fan, there are some lovely moments. Notably, the inclusion of the greatest Greg Lake piece ever — 'I Believe In Father Christmas', the single from a few Christmases ago. And Lake's other offering, 'Watching Over You', is a beaut. Without doubt, Lake could become a superstar in his own right if he ever left the band. Coupled with Emerson and Palmer, they offer some other good tracks — 'So Far To Fall' and 'Tiger In A Spotlight'. Emerson makes his presence felt on three other tracks, and for this album is in a honky-tonk piano mood. At times, I felt it was Russ Conway and not ELP. However, 'Barrelhouse Shake-Down' is a superb track and the best of the Emerson bunch. It is on the remaining tracks that the album falls down. In the past, an ELP album has kept its high standard throughout, but this one offers three poor tracks. However, with the high spots I have mentioned, the album should be quite well-received by loyal fans."

Another journalist writing for a local British newspaper, opined of *Works Volume 2*; "It surprised and relieved me to find that this single album bears little resemblance to the weighty, ostentatious *Volume 1*. The set offers an accurate, entertaining and unusually concise coverage of the many shades of ELP. Emerson's honky-tonk piano, Lake's ballads, complicated synthesised compositions, jazzy experiments and heavy basics. Some of the material, too, is familiar, with tracks like 'Brain Salad Surgery', 'I Believe In Father Christmas' and 'Honky Tonk Train Blues', plus an orchestral version of Scott Joplin's 'Maple Leaf Rag', and a new arrangement of the old favourite drinking song, 'Show Me The Way To Go Home'. The variety of the twelve tracks holds the attention in a way that *Volume 1* does not. But the album, for all its improvements, still underlines ELP's big fault, and that is lack of feeling. The music is technically excellent, but tracks like 'Bullfrog', with its jungle drums and bubbly sound effects, and the confusing 'So Far To Fall' will be bewildering to all but the most devoted ELP fans."

Under the heading of "LP Of Polished Self-Indulgence From ELP", another local British newspaper reviewed *Works Volume 2*; "Twelve tracks — none of which could be classed among the best the maestros have created. Even so, the group are typically self-indulgent, flamboyant and irresistible (to ELP aficionados at least). 'Tiger In A Spotlight', 'Bullfrog' and 'Brain Salad Surgery' all run together, but my personal favourites are the Keith Emerson tracks, 'Barrelhouse Shake-Down', 'Honky Tonk Train Blues', and Joplin's 'Maple Leaf Rag' (with the London Philharmonic). The production on all the tracks is by Greg Lake and is admirable, very full, and highly polished, which goes for ELP too, I suppose."

****

Both *Works* albums were supported with a tour. Spanning dates across 1977 and 1978, it featured the band playing with an orchestra on stage for some of the earlier dates. It was something that Emerson had aspired to for quite some time by that point. He had mentioned it even prior to ELP's performance at the Isle of White Festival in 1970: "My love of classical music is obviously something which is inherent as a musician, but I am not consciously inflicting it upon the new group. What I am, I am, and that some of our work may sound like classical rock is incidental rather than premeditated. It is possible we may use large orchestras in the future, but not this year. This year we want to establish the group identity."

Touring with an orchestra was a short-lived endeavour due to the financial demands of such extravagance. Consisting of around seventy musicians, although the concept of having an orchestra was exciting and innovative, it wasn't economic and, relatively early on in the tour, had to be scrapped

Emerson explained, "I've never been one to check on how much it would cost or how long it would last. Obviously I had a feeling that we couldn't afford to last out the tour with the orchestra. But it came as a bit of a shock when our manager walked in the dressing room one night before the show and said we had to stop the orchestra. We had to go out as a three-piece, there was no other choice. We had our manager with a shotgun behind us saying, 'Look, if you don't play as a three-piece, forget it, you'll be bankrupt'... I know what I like. Any artist knows their taste. We play rock 'n' roll really well. But we were at a stage in our career where just to play rock 'n' roll would have been very enjoyable but not serious enough. We enjoy rock 'n' roll. We could quite easily make a rock 'n' roll album at any time and enjoy it and get artistic rewards from it. Real ones. But when we stopped touring three years ago that wasn't a possible alternative. We could now."

Clearly, ELP were over-ambitious with regards to the scope of how far they could take their classical music aspirations. Emerson told *Gig* in September 1977; "Musically, it was like the bottom dropping out of my world when we had to drop the orchestra. I was very worried when we did the first gig without the orchestra because I thought the audience would feel cheated. In fact, they loved it. I was quite surprised because all the time I'd been thinking we've got to hit our audiences with something bigger and better. It came as a very encouraging shock when we discovered we really don't have to do all that; they'll love us anyway. That made me feel better."

Having cancelled the orchestra, Stewart Young said, "We knew from the beginning it would be a gamble. It would have been better to return to touring as a three-piece but we all wanted to do something that had never been done before. We're still having to pay for the orchestra because the union contract lasts until the end of July. We all met following the Des Moines show, and after an emotional discussion, the orchestra unanimously agreed to the change."

He added in later years; "I think the shows were successful, but at a certain stage it was too expensive. I went to the band and said, 'We're going to have to cut the orchestra, it's too big'. We had a meeting with the orchestra and told them about this, and everyone was quite upset, and a lot of them came to me and said they were having a fantastic time, and could they continue if we didn't pay them. But there are union rules, and unfortunately you can't do that in America."

"It's not all lost with the orchestra," said Palmer in 1977. "We've already accomplished two important things. The orchestra contributed to more than just the live performance. We got a live album out of the first concerts in Montreal Olympic Stadium, with the orchestra. And there will be a film of those concerts. So we've gained from the relationship. We will appear with an orchestra again in the future."

Having to lose the orchestra probably wasn't all that bad. Lake recalled; "When we did 'Fanfare For The Common Man' live, we'd all play along and it would all sort of blend, as most things would. What you often get with bands when they play with orchestras is this terrible lagging of time and this delay, because orchestral instruments tend to speak late. And, of course, orchestras are not used to playing in time. They really couldn't play in time at all with us, so in the end we had to play in time with them. We had to follow the conductor which was a bit unnerving. The whole of your life you're used to coming in on time, and all of a sudden you find that beat number one is actually halfway to beat number two. And you have to delay your instinct to play, which is very unnerving — I found it very difficult, personally. The conductor really did the very best that he could, but the thing is instruments like French horns, they just don't react that quickly. Whereas the piano or guitar reacts straight away, no delay."

"It would be true to say that Keith was driving this orchestral route," he added. "He felt some desire to be recognised for his classical musicianship, and I think that he really felt that that was something that was going to be established by performing with orchestras. Whereas I was personally keener on making innovative music as a three-piece band."

Perhaps Emerson's house fire had made the keyboard player think in a more blasé way than he might otherwise have done. "I lost a lot of music and didn't care about anything for months — just stayed drunk most of the time," he explained before the tour. "Finally I was able to vent my frustration. I learned not to place much value on anything I buy because of the fire — this tour, for instance. If we lose money, so what? Just so I'm satisfied aesthetically. There's no way we can make money."

Prior to the tour, the plan was that as well as the orchestra (and the usual road crews, sound crews and personal assistants, plus caterers and accountant), other travelling companions in the entourage would be a doctor and Carl Palmer's karate teacher. Each band member was into physical fitness and ensured to exercise daily. As part of a similar level of self-care, the only hotels on the itinerary were those with full health facilities and twenty-four-hour room service. Lake remarked that moving ELP was not too dissimilar to having to move a small town. Whilst the tour was looking to be a fifty-date one, he also enthused, "That's the number of stops so far, but I don't think that will be the end of it." At this stage, he stated that he estimated the whole thing would cost "in the region of four-million, maybe five-million" dollars.

Much of the operation was to be handled by many of the same people who were used to working out logistics of a similar scale and complexity for the Royal Ballet of Canada. The colossal scale of the tour was representative of a huge risk for ELP; in particular, until the release of *Works Volume 1*, the band had been out of sight and out of mind for a good few years by then. An American journalist also considered the point that "With ELP, the problem is compounded by the fact that their music is not basic boogie, but a complex combination of classical and rock".

The band were certainly not ignorant to the gamble they were taking. "We're risking our necks by going into so much so soon with the big album and the tour," Lake admitted. "But we've got to come back and be present in the world. We haven't been around, and at the moment, we're not hot. We've got to get hot again. There are slower, safer ways. But if this works, people will be astounded."

And as the *Chicago Tribune* considered in May 1977, "*Works Volume 1* has sold briskly enough (more than a million copies were shipped out to record stores) and is climbing high on the charts."

In preparation for the tour, where it had been estimated that three-million people would be paying to see them perform, the band spent the majority of three months rehearsing with the orchestra and chorus in Montreal. It had been chosen for its good facilities and, perhaps more importantly, the Royal Ballet crew was headquartered there. Rehearsal sessions throughout this period mostly took up a whole day. There was a clear reason for it though: "We're doing a two-and-a-half-hour show and there's a lot of music to go over," Lake explained. "Playing a concert is a more nerve-wracking experience than just releasing an album. We're conscious of the fact that it has been a long time since we've played. We realise it's not going to be a matter of just walking back in. Obviously, we're interested in how the tour's going to turn out."

"We'll have all of our electronic wizardry at hand," he promised. "And a little fairy dust too. As for how the orchestra will be received, well, when we released our version of Mussorgsky's *Pictures At An Exhibition* five years ago, people were apprehensive then too. They wondered how that would be received by our audience; it was such a long classical piece and all. But it turned out to be one of the most popular things we've done, in America, at least. So I don't think the classical colourings are bad things. They're hard to get exposure on as far as airplay goes, but they're very powerful in a live context. I don't think anyone's going to be disappointed with our show. I think it'll be an overwhelming experience. That's why we're doing it."

Vitally, despite how some critics would go on to regard the use of an orchestra as excessive, ELP wasn't just doing it in order to make a grand statement, for of course, sonically, the use of an orchestra was about the music that they wished to create. "We stopped touring because we felt we'd gone down one path long enough and were wearing it out," Lake said of the band's earlier hiatus. "We had reached the end of the road electronically, and we had to have some time to think, to recreate, to decide what we wanted to do. We felt we had to go in a different direction. For us, that turned out to involve playing with acoustic instruments, playing with an orchestra to get the effects we wanted that electronics alone couldn't give us."

When performances on the tour were reviewed, whilst some critics considered that the use of an orchestra was overzealous, others complained that the orchestra's absence was problematic. Overall though, orchestra or no orchestra, most of the reviews of ELP's performances were overwhelmingly positive — both in terms of the group's musicianship, and in terms of their ability to captivate an audience. Sure, some complained that ELP's approach to being on stage was perhaps, at times, a little cold and mechanical, but really, it could be argued that the nature of their act had always been one to demand that they focus rather than take time out to schmooze over the audience's presence.

Interestingly, when speaking to a journalist in October 1977, Palmer admitted that with the band having been away for a while, it had been harder for them to sell tickets to some of the venues. "We had toured every year for six years prior to taking three years off," he said. "The actual comeback to touring was difficult, but nothing that time can't sort out. The physical and mental effects are noticeable, but I enjoy staying in a different hotel room every night. That's the spirit of touring. That's the fun of it all."

The Indianapolis News reported in June 1977; "If Emerson, Lake and Palmer's five-million-dollar tour is to survive to the end, it will have to draw more people than it did last night at Market Square Arena. Right now, ELP stands for expertise, lavishness and professionalism, but it could need H.ELP (sic) at the turnstiles to survive its fifty-city tour. Not even half a full house (an estimate of eight-thousand just probably stretching it) showed up for the poshly produced concert and enjoyed what it saw and heard. It's likely the general admission festival seating format hurt the show at the gate. The post-college crowd simply won't fight the school kids for the good seats. They would rather plunk down their ten dollars and have a seat waiting for them at eight, instead of standing in line outside and rushing for a spot when the gates open at seven. If anything, the show was slightly overdone. An orchestra and a choir are nice, but is it necessary?

Everything You've Ever Dreamed

Synthesisers can do almost as much, and Keith Emerson, a pioneer of the funny keyboards, knows it. Imagine what it costs to house and feed this travelling city of sight and sound, not to mention the quibbling over who shares rooms with whom."

"Needless to say, the show was polished, almost blinding. Six stages stacked upon the main stage housed the orchestra. More than two-hundred overhead floodlights, three banks above the stage and one near the middle of the hall, provided more than enough colour. Emerson thrashed away at a Yamaha GX1 keyboard and polysynthesiser, which looks like a glorified Ma Bell switchboard, complete with an oscilloscope, a digital readout, flashing lights and miles of wires. Once the board popped and smoked and finally "exploded" before disappearing into the stage. Drummer Carl Palmer attacked his rotating monogrammed drum and percussion setup with passion, while the quiet, round-faced Greg Lake peacefully played his guitars and uttered crisp golden sounds. There weren't too many bad seats in the house. Since the stage supported so much equipment (the most ever at the arena), the crowd was situated further west in the oval than usual. Those sitting down got to see the trio in closer perspective, but didn't benefit from the full sound and overall effect of the production as those in the back and upper chairs did. The sound was above par for the most part, in spite a couple of mysterious pops and crashes and one instance of feedback."

"Each orchestra member was mic'd and sometimes drowned out the choir. It happened disappointingly during Lake's vocals and acoustic guitar playing on 'From The Beginning'. Following Lake's beautiful 'C'est La Vie', the group closed the first set with a slightly reworked version of *Pictures At An Exhibition.* One standing ovation. Emerson, sucking on a bottle of expensive wine, opened the second set with a watered-down version of his original 'Piano Concerto No.1' from his side of the current *Works Volume 1* album. Two standing ovations. The low-keyed Lake took his turn by performing 'Closer To Believing' and 'Lucky Man'. He missed a chord on 'Lucky Man', but got standing ovation number four regardless. Next up in the parade was the jersey'd Palmer and his infamous 'Tank' drum solo. Midway through the riff, Palmer's platform did a 180-degree turn to flashing strobes. He also turned and pounded on a set of kettle drums while the guys at the soundboard played electronic tricks with the vibrations. Another stand-up shout."

It was reported in the Newport *Daily Press* in July 1977; "Emerson, Lake and Palmer will be appearing at the Scope Saturday night on their first tour in three years. The group's *Works* album will be the focal point of the show, which will run approximately two-and-three-quarter hours.

The group was using a seventy-piece orchestra on every day of the tour. Keyboard player Rick Wakeman mounted a similar venture, and all but bankrupted himself in the process. I spoke to ELP's bassist and vocalist Greg Lake Thursday afternoon and he filled me in on the group's reasons for limiting the use of the symphony orchestra to thirty-or-forty-thousand-seat arenas. 'We haven't dropped the orchestra completely. We will be using it at Madison Square Garden and the Olympic Stadium in Montreal.' They couldn't afford to use it on the smaller dates. The band did nine concerts with the orchestra and on June 12th stopped using it in order to circumvent economic suicide. 'It was costing us $200,000 a week for the symphony orchestra. We already had $1,500,000 of our own money invested in the project.' Lake said the group had to raise ticket prices for the tour in order to make things work out in their favour. 'We haven't made any money in three years.' Lake said the group decided to restrict the use of the seventy-member aggregation to venues that could pay for it. Needless to say, Norfolk Scope is not one such venue. Lake said limiting use of the orchestra turned out to have a few advantages for the musicians in that it loosened things up a bit. The group was required to keep the music under tight control when using the orchestra arrangements. The boys have regained a little independence without it, and can experiment and improvise with or without the orchestra. One can be sure the concert will be first-rate. 'We regret the loss, but we are realists,' says Lake. It's easy to see why."

The *Binghamton Press* reported in July 1977; "There were really four stars at the Emerson, Lake and Palmer concert last night at the Veterans Memorial Arena. Three of the stars were, of course, Keith Emerson, Greg Lake and Carl Palmer. The fourth was a stage that was a technological wonder. It did practically everything but send out ELP's laundry. Musically, it was a superb show with one irritating exception: nary a word of Emerson's introductions or Lake's lyrics could be clearly heard. I talked with people who are knowledgeable about sound, and they tell me that the steel and concrete structure of the arena makes it difficult to get the crystal-clear sound that a group is able to get inside a recording studio, particularly if the group emphasises instrumentals instead of vocals. Well, I'd buy that except for one thing. If a group such as ELP can bring five truckloads of equipment and tonnes of speakers, control boards and sound equipment, it seems the gang of technicians skittering around during the performance could figure out a way to adjust for the vocal passages. About the only Lake vocal I heard clearly was the romantic 'C'est La Vie', accompanied only by an acoustic guitar and Emerson's accordion. Yes, an accordion. Emerson is probably the only rock star alive who can get away with playing an accordion. He could probably even play 'Lady Of Spain' on it and not get laughed off the stage. Emerson showed himself to be a great rock keyboard player. Certainly the best I've ever heard in concert. You'd have to go far to find anyone else who has such mastery over such a wide range of keyboard instruments, plus a colossal panel of electronic gadgetry that he manages like the Wizard of Oz. His variety is also stunning. From Jimmy Smith-type jazz, to Jerry Lee Lewis rockabilly, to classical. The group didn't bring any side musicians with them, but they were quite capable of creating a gigantic sound by themselves."

"Palmer is a good drummer. I'd even say great except that I got the feeling he was a bit too incessant. There was a sort of monotony to his high-voltage performance, although his lengthy solo during the end of the one-hundred-minute set was terrific. Now, about the stage: It was a two-level affair with Palmer's drums perched at least fifteen feet above the floor. The drums sat on a rotating stage, so when he played, the drums would revolve a full 360 degrees. If that was spectacular, it was nothing compared to Emerson's gadgets. He had a portable keyboard that shot off flares, a grand piano that rose from the depths of the stage, and a control panel that exploded with appropriate fireworks and smoke. Emerson isn't subtle. He also was no slouch as a pianist. He performed part of his 'Piano Concerto No.1', which is on the two-record *Works* album, and showed himself to be as well versed in classical structure as he is in rock. Classical rock has been a hallmark of the group, and they have suffered some criticism for it. *The New York Times*, for example, has termed them pretentious for trying to meld rock with the classics. But I found it exciting when they played Aaron Copland's 'Fanfare For The Common Man' and Tchaikovsky's *Nutcracker* suite. It may not have been suitable for classical purists, but it was exciting entertainment. The ELP concert last night marked the fifth consecutive rock concert to sell out the arena. There were slightly over seven-thousand paid admissions."

In July 1977, under the heading of "ELP Sans Band — Still A Classy Show", the *Democrat & Chronicle* reported; "'The wave of the future is not in smash-bang! Nor is it in electronics. It is in musical expression. And just as we once opened doors for other groups electronically, we're now going to do it musically.' Those are the words of Greg Lake of Emerson, Lake and Palmer, in a recent *Rolling Stone* interview. Lake was speaking several weeks ago, as ELP prepared to launch their first major tour in more than three years, a tour on which the three-man British rock group was to be accompanied by a seventy-piece symphony orchestra. By the time the tour rolled into Rochester's War Memorial Saturday night, however, economics had forced ELP back to its original three-man format. The orchestra was dropped from the tour after several less-than-sold-out concerts in the mid-west. Without their orchestral support, ELP didn't open any musical doors Saturday, but they put on a solid classy performance before seven-thousand fans. It was much in the vein of the shows they were doing when they stopped performing back in 1974."

"Not surprisingly, keyboard wizard Keith Emerson was the focal point of ELP's Rochester concert. Emerson, who came to ELP by way of The Nice, is probably the single person most responsible for the popularity of synthesisers among today's rock groups. Saturday night, Emerson showed that the man who was once a pioneer in the field of electronic rock music is still one of the leaders. Playing grand piano as well as innovative synthesisers and electronic keyboards, Emerson went a long way towards making up for the absence of the orchestra. At one point, with Lake and Palmer setting up a jazz-style rhythmic framework, Emerson used one hand to play lead on an electric organ, while supplying riffs and fills from a synthesiser with the other hand. The end result was a three-man group sounding like something out of the big band era — with Emerson's synthesiser, taking the place of the brass section."

"While Emerson was in the spotlight, much of the time guitarist Greg Lake and percussionist Carl Palmer were given their own segments of the show. Lake came up with some nice versions of his acoustic ballads, such as 'Lucky Man', 'Still... You Turn Me On' and 'C'est La Vie'. An excellent speaker system, which was purchased for this tour, allowed Lake's acoustic guitar to be heard without distortion, even when being played along with Emerson's electronic instruments. In addition to their music, which still sounded fresh in spite of the age of much of the material, ELP augmented the show with some dynamic and tasteful lighting and a futuristic-but-simple stage setup. Palmer's drums were set up on a chromium-framed platform, which evolved 180 degrees during his solo on 'Tank' to reveal a set of copper kettle drums and a pair of huge gongs painted with Chinese-style dragons. Emerson, Lake and Palmer may no longer be the group of the future as they once were, but they are still capable of producing two hours of compelling and varied music."

Under the heading of "ELP Plus Entourage Is Less Than Equal", the *Asbury Park Press* considered in July 1977; "Emerson, Lake and Palmer show that they still work best in concert as just E, L and P. The band says it risked its life earnings to carry the entourage for full orchestral backing on songs from its new album, *Works Volume 1*. But transportation costs ran high and after several non-sell-outs, ELP jettisoned the orchestra at dates in Philadelphia, New Haven and most other cities. A three-night stand with the orchestra in New York, however, indicated that fans in the other cities missed little. While the orchestra was needed on Emerson's twenty-five-minute 'Piano Concerto No.1', the audience's subdued reaction to the serious classical piece suggested the massive undertaking was for naught. Keith Emerson, Greg Lake, and Carl Palmer spent three years away from the concert stage to finish the new double album on which each band member takes control of one side, with the fourth side consisting of a joint effort. When they finally ended the concert hiatus and mounted the huge, clean-looking stage at Madison Square Garden, they were greeted by a barrage of camera flashes that surpassed the band's own stage lighting. Opening with 'Hoedown', they energetically ran through a medley of old hits from their *Brain Salad Surgery*, *Tarkus* and *Pictures At An Exhibition* albums before taking a break to set up Emerson's long solo piece. The orchestra, however unnecessary, blended easily with the older songs, especially since ELP earned its reputation by taking classical themes from Copland, Mussorgsky, and Prokofiev and reworking them in a rock framework. Any such undertaking opens an artist to complaints from traditionalists, and American critics have been especially harsh in evaluating Emerson's concerto, with one calling it 'almost gauche enough to be camp'."

"One of the toughest things for a band in concert is to weave in new material without boring a crowd eager to hear the old hits. ELP does this better than most bands. Following the hour-long set of oldies and Emerson's solo piece, the band skilfully mixed selections from Lake and Palmer's solo sides with older songs like 'Lucky Man', 'Nut Rocker' and 'Knife-Edge'. The band also was brave enough to encore with a new song, Copland's 'Fanfare For The Common Man', one of the best cuts on the new album. Here the orchestral horns added a regal opening touch as the band expanded Copland's short piece into a fifteen-minute romp that brought the audience to its feet."

"The audience response to the new material was generally as good as to the old. At the end of several songs, an excited and nervous Keith Emerson repeatedly yelled, 'Was it really that good?' prompting the crowd to scream even louder. The band's music was as complex and intricate as ever. ELP has no electric guitarist and Emerson, who introduced synthesisers to the rock world seven years ago, is forced to play the lead melodies. Lake fills in on acoustic guitar and bass, while Palmer handles rhythm chores on drums. The mixture of hard rockers with softer acoustic songs like 'Still... You Turn Me On' generally went well, although Lake's schmaltzy 'C'est La Vie' lacked only an accordion to make it prime material for *The Lawrence Welk Show*."

"Palmer is one of the few drummers who can begin a drum solo without eliciting groans from a bored audience. His reworked version of 'Tank' was short, tasty and accompanied by excellent synchronised lighting effects. But the effects thankfully were held to a minimum compared to the technological wonders used by groups like Pink Floyd that tend to overshadow the music. ELP was one of the first all-star "supergroups" to emerge in the early seventies. With Emerson coming from The Nice, Lake from King Crimson, and Palmer from Atomic Rooster. They say they recorded *Works Volume 2* while cutting their current album, so fans won't again have to wait several years for a follow-up release."

In August 1977, the *Vancouver Province* opined; "The standard criticisms levelled at Emerson, Lake and Palmer invariably have to do with pretension, excess and indulgence — not surprisingly, since ELP are usually guilty of all three, with a vengeance. Their tendency to favour technology *uber alles*, for promoting style and sonic mayhem over substance, and for generally disregarding any semblance of taste or restraint, both on record and in performance, approaches legendary proportions. There are those who've spent several years revering them for those dubious and diabolical qualities; there is an equal contingent that has vilified the group on the same grounds. The latter category has always suited me just fine. Their only truly impressive Vancouver appearance to date was the last one in 1974, when the production matched the musical monomania blow for blow, managing to effectively hammer artistic reservations into submission with total, no-holds-barred mechanical magnificence."

"Their show at the Coliseum on Saturday night, however, was spectacular in a whole other way. It wasn't that ELP had abandoned any of its computerised glory: Carl Palmer still drums as if he were controlled and energised by some superhuman programmer, Greg Lake still delivers his bass lines with the same indestructible sense of fatalism. Keith Emerson plays his arsenal of keyboards and synthesisers as if terminally obsessed by a vision of a futuristic man-machine confrontation in which he is the last human gladiator. But for the first time, the group demonstrated an ability to edit and discipline itself, to dispense with unnecessary trash-flash in favour of clean, well-defined concepts and intelligent, though still exceptionally powerful, thematic development — to acknowledge tactics as well as technology."

"Perhaps the financial foiling of their enormously ambitious plan to carry a seventy-piece orchestra around with them across the continent forced some judicious restructuring: having one's most grandiose vision proved impractical is unavoidably humbling. But whatever the reason, the performance — stripped down, focused, unprecedentedly to the point — was nothing short of superb. Visually aided by a few well-timed flash pots and explosions, exemplary use of lighting (and culminating with Emerson's *de rigueur* one-on-one battle with an organ), the show built to a progressive series of climaxes with deadly accuracy, the interest level maintained not only by a decibel barrage, but by dramatic shifts in tone — a heretofore undeveloped understanding of dynamics that the group has now mastered flawlessly. Emerson's lunatic synthesiser work on the classics was tempered by some sensitive, highly romanticised passages on acoustic grand, Palmer's awesome motor-muscular bouts with his huge revolving drum stand balanced by Lake's finely-groomed moments of clean, acoustic guitar-accompanied vocals — in all, a performance that quite outdid anything ELP has managed before. A superlative performance: one that not only vindicated the fidelity of the group's already legion fans, but is bound to have made a whole new set of converts."

In August 1977, the *San Francisco Examiner* considered of the performance that had taken place at the Cow Palace; "ELP are definitive robot-rock, showing little emotion or interest in their whereabouts or audience. This image, of course, fits in well with the technology of their act — Palmer must have a dozen mics on his drums, cymbals, timpani, gongs, vibes, glockenspiel, etc. Emerson has at least six keyboards, mostly electronic, and Lake's vocals, with acoustic guitar or electric bass, are precision-balanced to fit into the auditorium sound system. Emerson has real piano chops, weaving synthetic sounds as well as grand piano embroidery through all the numbers; he and Palmer often do it in a way similar to the Chick Corea and Billy Cobham jazz combinations. It's all very showy, and turns occasionally, towards monotony. The canon (a pair) shoots off three rounds apiece during 'Pirates', which is a first-rate story song."

In August 1977, a journalist writing for a local American newspaper enthused; "No one should go through life without having seen Emerson, Lake and Palmer in concert at least once. After all, where also could one witness a) a man enveloped in a golden array of rotating drums, b) a musical composition which calls for an exploding computer for percussion, c) someone playing an organ while the instrument lies flat on top of him, and d) that very same organ spun on one leg until the entire electronic body comes crashing to the stage in an unceremonious mass of feedback. Oh, yes, the music was rather entertaining too. Performing a two-hour-plus set at the Long Beach Arena, Emerson, Lake and Palmer offered what seemed to be a hastily compiled set, gearing heavily on compositions from the group's three earliest albums. Because of problems of a massive expense, the orchestra and choir did not appear for the Los Angeles appearances. The hasty cancellation for this area, and most of the North American tour, would be the likely explanation for the quickly assembled programme. In addition, certain songs, particularly those from the brilliant new album *Works Volume 1*, cried for orchestration. 'C'est La Vie', Greg Lake's composition, and the excerpts performed from Keith Emerson's 'Piano Concerto No.1' were examples. But in spite of the problems — which were understandable and inevitable, under the circumstances — ELP proved that talent didn't dissipate with the two-and-a-half-year hiatus. On the contrary, only the hasty arrangements were weak; their individual and collective talents were very, very strong."

"One of the more specific downfalls with the evening's arrangements was that many of the pieces were abridged unnecessarily. The opening selection was 'Karn Evil 9: 1st Impression — Part 2', handsome yet far more powerful when performed in the context of the entire work. 'Tarkus', from their second album, was also shortened, as was *Pictures At An Exhibition*, the bastardisation of Mussorgsky's classical piece. It too, pleaded for the contrasting smoothness of an orchestra, as had been the case in some East Coast concerts."

"The wizardry of Carl Palmer resurrected the original version of 'Tank' from the first ELP release, and showed he is virtually the only rock drummer who can get away with an eight-minute drum solo and not lose the attention of the audience. Greg Lake, the weakest performer of the three, employed the clearest, sharpest voice in rock music to highlight 'C'est La Vie', 'Still... You Turn Me On' and 'Lucky Man' among others. But Emerson is a magician. He grabs the attention from the opening of the concert and never lets go — from the parading with a Moog ribbon attachment in 'Hoedown', to the exploding of a computer bank in *Pictures*, to the well-earned encore of Aaron Copland's 'Fanfare For The Common Man'. His finest moment though, was the excerpts from his 'Piano Concerto No.1' (incorporated into the stirring 'Take A Pebble'). Emerson is a musician first and an entertainer second; he does both with a prowess beyond comparison. But if one were to have the audacity to try to classify ELP, they could be called the thinking man's Kansas. ELP do not perform bombast; they perform carefully calculated compositions. On the next tour, perhaps they will be better prepared and not be thrust into a surprise situation."

In February 1978, writing for a local newspaper of the performance that took place at Princeton University, the journalist opined; "Emerson, Lake and Palmer performed with opera-like virtuosity. Their control of the instruments, techniques and technologies was cool, short and inspired. The audience saw masters of their individual crafts exhibiting where they have taken, and have been led by, their music and each other since their last concert tour... All band members played the usual solo for a time and then played and jammed together in various combinations. A melodic theme of classical origin would be reworked through jazz, honky-tonk, boogie, rock, and ELP rhythms. They know, and so now do the concert goers, that they have the ability to play well whatever type of music they wish, and incorporate whatever technology they can create. Their style is one of control, practice, planning and stalled exuberance."

In March 1978, a journalist writing for a local American paper reported; "Watching Emerson, Lake and Palmer perform is like witnessing a time trip, to use a tattered metaphorical cliché. Spaced-out baroque, so to speak. They take you back to the seventeenth century, to the end of the renaissance, and materialise you in a cathedral resplendent with the frescoes of the masters. You can almost see a gigantic ancient organ filling the ornate halls with energetic climactic improvisation. Mad. Passionate."

"Last week's show at Freedom Hall proved that the masters of baroque have not died. They have been reincarnated in the form of Keith Emerson. The "rock 'n' roll" keyboard player already has his concertos performed by the Montreal Symphony Orchestra and others. Despite his historically-entrenched style, Emerson's music is still too avant-garde for many conductors, though. Emerson has that paradoxical quality. His music is a fluid continuum from the past that reaches into the future. As the concert last week began, a sophisticated-appearing apparatus with a conglomerate of illuminated terminals, digital readouts, and video oscillation screens slowly rose from below the stage, reminiscent of the monolith from *2001*. Emerson, frail and tall, chewing gum, like a computer engineer from the future, looks on, his fingers flying across the keyboards of his synthesiser. You wonder if he is lord or slave to his musical machines."

"Greg Lake is walking his bass in a driving repetition while Carl Palmer, who resembles a weightlifter, is all over his drums. Two huge gongs, which look like they could have belonged to the Incas, are on each side. Emerson is flying through an improvisation previously unrecorded, looking very relaxed until he senses that it is beginning to drag. Then he is at his synthesiser in earnest, dispelling any doubts about what is in store for the audience. The group goes through 'Tarkus', 'Pirates' and 'Tank' and you realise why ELP are called the smallest symphony orchestra in the world. But their music is mechanical, and I worried about electricity's threat to acoustic music."

"Boom! The sound is deafening. Smoke is pouring out of the "monolith" and the oscillators have given away to a single straight line. Another loud explosion. The machine — seemingly worth several-thousand dollars — is consumed in the smoke of its melting circuits. It slowly descends to below the stage again, true to the theme of *Tarkus*, one of their earliest albums. The machine is vanquished. It is the servant. ELP disappears from the stage and an English chap announces that there will be a brief intermission before the group returns. The audience was ecstatic. Before the concert was over, ELP were to receive a standing ovation after every number. ELP stage two was even better than before. In this set, each musician performs a solo, true to the concept of *Works 1* where each member recorded one album side themselves. Greg Lake, diamond earring shimmering in his right ear, had the women swooning. He is playing twelve-string guitar, singing 'C'est La Vie', 'Lucky Man' and 'Still... You Turn Me On'. I look over at my wife. She looks like what she must have looked like at her first Beatles concert."

"Emerson does his piano concertos and proves that the synthesiser has not ruined his abilities, like it has hurt Herbie Hancock. On the acoustic piano, he is as skilled as anyone with his lengthy musical training. Seeing either he or Lake alone would have warranted the cost of a ticket. Then it is Palmer's turn. I generally hate drum solos because they quickly become tedious and monotonous. Not so here. Palmer showed that each member of the group is geared towards perfection. He wears his hair short, like Slowhand Clapton, another perfectionist in the world of modern music individualists. He and his drums are on a revolving mini stage turned, he said in an earlier press conference, 'by slaves'. He said it once operated mechanically and suddenly during a concert stopped while he was pointed with his back to the audience. The lighting from above and below the drums is dazzling, nearly as good as his percussion. A contact pickup connects his drums to a synthesiser and he actually has a melody with his beats. The audience is spellbound as he sounds first like something from ancient Africa and then like a musician from another galactic system. Palmer, like Lake sang in an earlier song, is on the 'wings of time'. So was everyone else."

For their *Works* albums and performances thereof, it is endearing that ELP didn't divert from the music they wanted to do when commercially, there were so many other genres that they could have latched on to. In August 1977, one journalist considered; "In a music world crazed with the rhythmic rotes of the disco clones and creamed with the syrup of homogenised Californian harmonies, the cool and calculated barons of English art rock, Emerson, Lake and Palmer, continue to march to the same rigid and precise steps that have taken them through seven years of progressive rock success." In many ways though, that was all about to change.

7.
I'm Moving Out Of Here

Love Beach was ELP's final seventies studio album, released prior to their evidential split the following year. By the end of their 1977–1978 North American tour, dynamics within the band were already strained. However, they were still under contractual obligation to make one more album. Retreating to Nassau in The Bahamas as tax exiles, ELP recorded *Love Beach* with lyricist Peter Sinfield — he is credited as a co-writer on each track. Once Lake and Palmer had finished recording their parts for the album, they left the island; Emerson was left to finish the album himself.

ELP had made it clear that they wanted to rest but they were encouraged by Ahmet Ertegun, the president of Atlantic Records, to record a new album. Ertegun didn't hesitate to remind the group that they had to deliver one more album. Emerson recalled a meeting where Ertegun strongly urged the group to make "a commercial album". From the very start, Emerson was reluctant about the idea. Lake recalled that Ertegun threatened to decline the band the prospect of solo albums if they refused to work together. With little say in the matter, ELP complied.

"The band had actually broken up when *Love Beach* was being recorded," Palmer explained. "Ahmet Ertegun came along and asked if we'd give it one more go. We said, 'Okay, but we've been touring for the last seven or eight years and we're fried!' People wanted to take time off, but we ended up in The Bahamas. Keith had bought a house there and Greg had bought one in conjunction with our manager at the time. I didn't own anything there, I just had a speedboat, which I eventually sold, of course! But I remember being there and Ahmet saying, 'Guys, chill out down here and I'll set up the studio'. That's how we dealt with it really. It was very laid-back. If you wanted one more album out of us at that point, the business people probably thought that it was the only way it was going to happen. I'm surprised it's not more reggae-sounding, because that could easily have happened!"

"I think at that time we would've gladly taken a break from touring and recording," Lake explained. "And because we were pressured into that situation, I think it was something where we all would've rather said, 'Look, we've gotta stop this for a while'. And that's really what happened. It just didn't feel right. It was one of those things. You'd have had to have been there at the time, but you could've felt it: nobody was that keen to play."

Advantageously, working on a commercial album suited Lake's method of songwriting. Having already written 'Lucky Man', he wasn't out of his comfort zone in that regard. Emerson however, admitted that he "eased up on my opinions to an extent, bit my nails, and gave him the freedom he kept asking for on side one". And of course, this all makes sense in view of the fact that really, following their hiatus in 1974, Emerson, Lake and Palmer hadn't actually done that much writing together, for the majority of *Works Volume 1* and *Works Volume 2* feature tracks where the band composed independently of each other.

Recording took place in 1978 at Compass Point Studios without a dedicated producer. Despite Lake having produced ELP's previous albums, when the recording of *Love Beach* began, nobody had been assigned to the role. Early pressings of the album didn't even express a producer's credit, but the mixing had largely been done by Emerson on the basis that he was the last of the trio to remain with the project when Lake and Palmer had left. The pressure was on; Emerson's increasing drug use had started to impair his ability to work well as part of a team.

Peter Sinfield had been asked by Stewart Young to join them in Nassau to assist Lake in writing the lyrics. Sinfield committed to the role but reluctantly so. He had his own frictions with Lake to the point that he insisted on being able to work alone.

Emerson was particularly unhappy with the album's title. It had been chosen by Atlantic Records — it had been taken from one of the album's songs by Lake and Sinfield that had been named after a stretch of beach on Nassau. The front cover photo was taken on an island off Salt Cay. Graphically, it was worlds apart from their previous albums up to that point; no longer did complex and intriguing artwork grace the album and instead, was a photograph of the band looking, not too unlike, as both Emerson and Palmer put it, the Bee Gees.

Emerson said; "I think it's the package that it kind of comes in. The most off-putting thing was that with ELP, we were basically looked upon as three very austere guys, you know? Back in those days, if you were photographed smiling and laughing, it didn't work. It was quite a long

I'm Moving Out Of Here

time before you saw The Beatles laughing. I think basically the package that *Love Beach* was put into, which had the three of ELP on the cover looking like the Bee Gees and having a good laugh — that was shock and horror."

Such was Emerson's uncertainty about the album that he organised a booth at Chicago's O'Hare International Airport to conduct a questionnaire on the public's opinion of it. When he reported back to Atlantic Records that many who took part in the survey were not impressed, the company still insisted on doing it their way and nothing was changed despite Emerson's research.

Love Beach was released in November 1978. Although Palmer spent two months trying to arrange a farewell tour, the ongoing tensions within ELP determined that it wasn't to be. Understandably, as well as being at a crossroads in terms of what to do musically, there was a sense of burn-out from years of touring. Besides, the pressure had been on to make *Love Beach* not only in and of itself, but in terms of how the record company had wanted to get it out relatively soon after the release of *Works Volume 2*.

Upon the release of *Love Beach*, what did ELP look like to someone who was unaware that the band would be going their separate ways for the foreseeable? Well, in January 1979, one journalist, perhaps rather rudely, noted; "Palmer, in town recently for the promotional duties, didn't come across like a cool rock veteran, but like an eager novice. In the coffee shop of the Century Plaza, he was trying hard to make this unusual situation seem like an everyday occurrence. However, he did admit after a while that ELP was currently making an effort to establish good media relations." To which Palmer was quoted; "We've never really been accessible to the media before because people haven't seen us in the papers much. We've got a reputation for being aloof, but we were aloof for too long. Some people have cultivated a negative image of us, in England, especially. There, they think of us as stuck-up and snooty."

The journalist continued; "ELP evidently needs publicity. The reason is that the band's record sales have declined drastically. In ELP's early-seventies heyday, a gold album — then indicating sales of a few 100,000 copies — was every artist's goal. The band earned six of them. These days when major pop artists commonly sell two-to-four-million copies of an album, ELP still has to struggle to surpass the 500,000 mark. *Works Volume 1* sold fairly well. But in Palmer's words, *Works Volume 2*, released for the Christmas season of 1977, is 'our worst-selling album ever'. At the moment at least, the new album doesn't seem to have enough pop appeal to reverse the slump. Buried in the flood of recent Christmas releases, *Love Beach* is floundering around the lower half of the top one-hundred, an embarrassing showing for a band of ELP's stature. The album desperately needs the support of a tour or hit single, something the band has never had. There won't be a tour for a while, Palmer reported, but the prospects of a hit single are brighter than usual. Usually, ELP's esoteric albums include little or nothing pop-oriented enough for AM radio, but *Love Beach* is a little different. One side is a typically long, intricate, grandiose suite that is unsuited for AM. The other side, however, features short, pop-oriented pieces, a rarity for an ELP album."

"Were these songs included to make the album more commercial? 'Of course not', Palmer replied rather huffily. 'We put in those shorter, more-condensed songs because we had never really done that. After *Works Volume 2*, we needed something different'. ELP's inexperience with short pop pieces is evident. These attempts at pop are actually threadbare, scaled-down progressive rock numbers. Right now, the trio lacks good pop instincts, but that's to be expected since pop is foreign territory for them. ELP is a victim of something it can't control: musical trends. Classical-style rock doesn't sell nearly as well as simple middle-of-the-road rock and Palmer is quite aware of this: 'Our music isn't for the man in the street. Generally, we haven't been into mass music. *Love Beach* is closer to mass music but it's still not mass music. Some of the *Love Beach* music is different for us. It's not really us'. ELP obviously is going through a difficult period of transition. They already have changed their attitude towards the press so what other concessions to the pop market are in store? How much are they willing to alter their music to attain commercial success? Palmer didn't have answers."

Ironically, perhaps a tour would have served to get *Love Beach* across to the record-buying public. Emerson considered with hindsight that the album might have had a better chance at success "if we'd gone out on the road and said, 'Forget what you've been listening to, this is the new direction'."

It could be said that commercially, ELP were in a particularly difficult position when it came to *Love Beach*. By 1978, the popularity of progressive rock had decreased significantly. The resulting situation arguably put ELP between a rock and a hard place. Had they decided to stay true to their trademark sound of long songs and complex arrangements throughout the album, they would have faced criticism for sounding dated. Alternatively, by opting for a more radio-friendly sound for the late-seventies, they ran the risk of alienating fans who turned out to be all too happy to label the band as sell-outs. With *Love Beach*, even if the band dynamics had not been strained by that point, in the wider context of the music that was popular by then, ELP couldn't win. After all, they weren't the only band who were at a crossroads in such regard, having thrived in the days when prog rock was at the peak of its popularity, and having to make vital decisions about where, creatively and commercially, they could make their sound appealing to the ever-changing market. If bands such as Yes, Genesis and Jethro Tull had to be mindful of such things, then certainly, ELP were no exception.

Having dedicated a full page spread to the excitement surrounding the release of Boney M's 1978 Christmas single, 'Mary's Boy Child', *The Daily Mirror* said simply of *Love Beach*; "Emerson, Lake and Palmer, remember them? Their sound is not unlike that of Yes. But Yes appear in public far more regularly than ELP."

"Genesis and Yes had successfully made that crossover," said Emerson in later years. "They'd had hit records. Atlantic Records were in the process of wanting to go that way — radio playable material was of all importance. What ELP had come up with before, the record company had to really go through it and say, 'What are we going to release as a single?'. We were not a singles band. *Love Beach* was an attempt to make a lot of radio playable material and to lighten up."

The album was reviewed in *Rolling Stone*; "*Love Beach* isn't simply bad, it's downright pathetic. Stale and full of ennui, this album makes washing the dishes seem a more creative act by comparison. Greg Lake contributes a handful of tediously standardised song forms while taking his three-chord arias and bel canto blues as haughtily as though he were singing lyrics by Guiseppe Verdi, not Peter Sinfield. Keith Emerson delivers another rip-off from the classics and a side-long ballad. Reduced to being a session player in his own band, the latter's accompaniments now sound like advertising jingles. Emerson's new meisterwork, 'Memoirs Of An Officer And A Gentleman', is more interesting than 'Pirates' was, but only because its composer has elected to work out the timbre changes on his keyboards rather than employ an elephantine orchestra again. Melodically, the tune is as vague as it is pompous; harmonically, it's a heap of sterile romantic clichés. That you can hear echoes of the ELP of old simply means that Emerson hasn't learned — or borrowed — a new riff in five years. Once more, Sinfield's lyrics are a grotesque embarrassment, probably accounting for Lake's wooden demeanour."

It is certainly plausible that the reviewer had never been a fan of ELP and their music. All the same though, Emerson later called *Love Beach* "an embarrassment against everything I've worked for".

Under the heading of "Washed Up On The Beach", one journalist opined; "The albums of Emerson, Lake and Palmer have seldom been consistent. But even on the worst albums, there were a few magic cuts.

Love Beach contains no magic cuts, only superficial wounds that are salted with poor production, mediocre musicianship and trite lyrics. Maybe the heat got to the talented trio while recording this disastrous disc in Nassau this past summer. Why else would Carl Palmer's usually powerful shot-from-guns drum sound be reduced to practice pad pitter-patter? Why else would Keith Emerson's wizardry at the keyboards lose all its magic? Why else would a reputable lyricist like Peter Sinfield strain with such benign rhymes as 'beating' and 'God's central heating'? Even the album's single sounds like third-rate Edgar Guest ('All I want is you/I'm on flight one-one-two'). It seems the band has gone purely commercial. In addition to the simplistic music, the evidence comes in the form of a full colour fold-out advertising all of ELP's previous albums on one side, and an order blank for *Love Beach* t-shirts, jogging shorts and satin jackets on the other. Think before you sink. Stay away from *Love Beach*."

Under the heading of "ELP Need Some Help", another journalist considered; "This is Emerson, Lake and Palmer's best studio album since 1974. But that's no reason for ELP fans to start rejoicing. The English trio's work since 1974 has not been distinguished. In place of the grandiose emptiness of *Works Volume 1*, or the hodgepodge nature of *Volume 2*, this LP contains six relatively modest group compositions and one classical interpretation. The upbeat 'All I Want Is You' is a convincing showcase for ELP's technical virtuosity. Greg Lake's vocal shines on the ballad, 'For You', and side two's lengthy suite, 'Memoirs Of An Officer And A Gentleman', is ELP's best extended work since 'Karn Evil 9' four years ago. Still, the band seems generally tired and outdated. It just doesn't have much to say anymore. And the extensive use of outside lyricist Pete Sinfield doesn't help matters any. *Love Beach* is a respectable, competent effort, but it contains none of the adventure, daring or ambition that marked *Brain Salad Surgery* or *Tarkus*. ELP could use either a shot of adrenaline or an early retirement."

From *Sounds*: "Really, I was willing to give this new ELP album every chance in the world, approach it with open ears, not to say an open mind. Why, I had even formulated some kind of a "defence" for the band, a sort of explanation as to why you should maybe still listen to them even though they may seem to represent the epitome of loaded superstars who know and care little about the life of the "lad on the street" and who think "UK Subs" is another term for England's soccer B-team. Yeah, I was prepared to ignore the awful cover (the disgustingly-tanned and healthy-looking ELP trio, posing like members of America on a beach in The Bahamas), lock away preconceived ideas and be generous, charitable, and kind-hearted. I wanted to give ELP a big chance, but they blew it.

I'm Moving Out Of Here

And *how*. No messin', no more beating about the bush. *Love Beach* is a dreadful album (and this comes from someone who was a big fan of this band around *Tarkus* and *Pictures At An Exhibition* days). Dreadful musically and *especially* lyrically."

"The facts: side one comprises six tracks. Four of them — 'All I Want Is You', 'Love Beach', 'Taste Of My Love' and 'For You' are love songs co-written by Greg Lake and "poet" Pete Sinfield and each is instantly dispensable. Sounding quite often like Foreigner outtake numbers, Lake rings every last drop of emotion out of such meaningful lyrics as 'You and me by the deep blue sea' and 'For you and I there never was a way to say goodbye' and everything consistently collapses into melodramatic rubble. Of the other two cuts, 'The Gambler' is an unconvincing story about a dice-throwin', poker-playin' dude and the inevitable "classicrock workout". 'Canario' skips spiritlessly along like a mediaeval-tinged 'In Dulce Jubilo' and unlike 'Fanfare For The Common Man' (from *Works Volume 1*) is definitely not the album's saving grace. Side two is the real pits however, a four-part conceptual work based around the 'Memoirs Of An Officer And A Gentleman'. Pete Sinfield, again has had a big hand in writing this, a sad but stirring tale of a fine upstanding man of the glory of doing battle for England! Over some unobtrusive but often quite flowery backing music, Lake gets all romantic and winces not in the slightest as he sings such appalling rhyming couplets as 'When I finally marched from Sandhurst, I learnt to put my fellow man first'."

The overall narrative surrounding *Love Beach* was that it was a dud, a blooper, a stain on ELP's discography up to and including that point — even for those who had been keen to support the band previously. Importantly though, it would be a missed opportunity to write it off entirely. For in recent years, it has been reappraised by fans across several different generations. ("It's funny," Palmer said a few years ago. "I've been saying that I don't like it, but people have been playing it and it's still on the radio in America! Listen, there are some good things on it. I just find it hard to believe that we called a prog album *Love Beach*!").

After all, it is still a point of interest for anyone who appreciates ELP's musical output overall. Not only does it show what they were able to create in the circumstances that were so against them at the time, but it also features some enjoyable music. Sure, it's not as complex as their older material but melodically it is memorable and from a musicianship and songwriting perspective, there is a lot to be embraced. And besides, even at the time, there were certainly people who welcomed the album favourably.

Writing for a local British newspaper, one journalist even considered

The ELP Story - *A Time and a Place*

that *Love Beach* signified what would be a comeback for ELP; "In the early days, their three-man setup of keyboards, bass and drums, blazed many a trail, producing gems like 'Lucky Man', 'Take A Pebble', 'Tank', *Trilogy*, *Pictures At An Exhibition*, 'Tarkus' and their masterpiece, 'Karn Evil 9'. Then came two ill-fated efforts in *Works Volumes 1 and 2*, which, apart from 'Pirates' and 'Fanfare For The Common Man', had little inspiration even though the idea of giving each member space for his own outlets was sound. However, with such grandiose exploits out of their collective systems, ELP set about getting back on the right road again, and as such, *Love Beach* proves to be their best album since *Brain Salad Surgery*. *Love Beach* will also surprise many diehard followers, for just as heavy rock is becoming popular again, ELP have tightened up and restrained their songs. The title track is probably the least effective track, with Greg Lake singing amiably about taking off in search of instant sunshine, but should prove to be a chart success anyway. But the band prove they can still rock as a collective unit, as witnessed on R&B cuts like 'Taste Of My Love', and 'Gambler'. And then there's side two of the record, totally devoted to the 'Memoirs Of An Officer And A Gentleman'. It takes some time getting used to, but this track should leave the door wide open for Keith, Greg and Carl to improvise their hearts out when played live. Overall, *Love Beach* marks the comeback for ELP as a magical force in the world of rock. Let's hope they stick to their origins and continue to climb back to that pinnacle which their own self-excess toppled them from such a long time ago."

Years later, Palmer said of the album, "I always refer to it as the worst album that ELP ever made. Not only did the music not really stand up for me, but the album cover, I didn't like. I didn't like the whole period of being in Nassau, The Bahamas. I didn't think that it was conducive to the band's way of writing, living, creating, rehearsing, playing... For me, it wasn't a great album, no." Critically though, he also considered; "To write a prog album, you've got to sit in traffic jams and go through a lot of shit before you get to the studio, and then you come up with the goods. When you're living in The Bahamas and you've got the beach and the sea and you've all got boats, what are you going to get? You're going to get *Love Beach*. But I will say that it does have 'Canario' by (Joaquin) Rodrigo, which was an idea of Keith's, and that's a fantastic piece of music."

With the advantage of hindsight, Lake's appraisal of *Love Beach* was perhaps the more balanced; "It's not that *Love Beach* is a bad album. It was an album that the band really didn't want to make. We were forced to make it contractually, but once we'd decided to do it, we gave it our best shot. So it was another ELP album, but it wasn't the best of ELP records — it wasn't *Tarkus*, *Trilogy*, *Brain Salad Surgery*, *Pictures At An Exhibition* or

Emerson, Lake and Palmer, or *Works Volume 1*. It wasn't that quality. It was an album that was tired creatively."

"When you've come from *Brain Salad Surgery* and *Tarkus*... America had got to us, obviously!" said Palmer.

In addition to negative reviews, *Love Beach* only got to number forty-eight in the UK and to number fifty-eight on the US Billboard 200. It spawned one single released in the UK, Lake and Sinfield's track, 'All I Want Is You'. Even supported by a performance on *Top Of The Pops*, it still floundered on the UK singles chart.

Cynically, a journalist wrote of the single for a local British newspaper; "Uninspired release following the successful 'Fanfare For The Common Man', no doubt destined for moderate chart success."

With *Love Beach* not being supported by a tour, in early 1979, ELP disbanded. "It wasn't like one of those break-ups where there was lots of mudslinging and bitterness," said Lake. "We all just felt simultaneously that we'd been pushed too far."

8.
Learning To Fly

Following the break-up of ELP, in 1979, Lake began to write new songs in preparation for his first solo album. He said he had "put down a tremendous amount of material". He travelled to Los Angeles to work with session musicians in order to further develop his songs. He was disappointed to find that, through no fault of the session musicians, the material lacked the spark that he was hoping for. This caused Lake to reconsider his approach; he concluded that he worked best as part of a committed group. As a result, he formed the Greg Lake Band.

The resulting album, *Greg Lake*, was released in September on Chrysalis Records. In both the UK and the US, the album only got to number sixty-two. The group's debut concert for the tour to promote the album was at the Reading Festival in the August of 1981. The line-up consisted of Gary Moore on guitar, Ted McKenna on drums, Tommy Eyre on keyboards, and Tristram Margetts on bass. A performance that took place at the Hammersmith Odeon in 1981 was broadcast live on the *King Biscuit Flower Hour* and was released as a live album in 1995.

At the time, Lake spoke pragmatically of what it meant to have left ELP — not from a personnel perspective, but in terms of the music. On balance, he made some good points about what it was that had put some people off ELP's music (as *New Musical Express* had put it in 1973, "ELP have always been one of those bands to provoke sharp differences in opinion. They win polls with immaculate ease. Commercially they're one of the world's biggest. Yet they're still often presented in print as a sort of soulless juggernaut, a lumbering musical monster.").

The freedom of being away from ELP afforded Lake the scope to be more candid about the whole thing: "It's no good staying together just for the sake of making as much money as you can, even though things are bad," he said. "It's okay for a while, but then you start feeling like a prostitute, selling yourself. I'm not saying I'm all that noble. I like money as much as the next guy, but I'll only go so far to make a buck." Also; "People expect my music to sound like ELP's. It doesn't. My solo album is rock 'n' roll, and very accessible. You can't call this pretentious or highbrow. This isn't ELP music. I'm through with that."

"I feel that some of the criticism levelled against us was justified," he said. "And I've tried to act upon it. We were perhaps pretentious at times, but at least we got out there and *did something*. I know some found it offensive that we were playing Mussorgsky, that we'd fucked with somebody's piano concerto. But I don't think we hurt anybody. Perhaps we even did a little good. The bottom line is that you don't have to buy a record or go to a show. You can turn off the radio, easily enough. It's a matter of free choice. And if you have a hit that people like, that's what matters. I consider myself very fortunate that I'm in a business where the buyer can take it or leave it."

And really, after the way in which *Love Beach* had been panned, who could blame him? Not only that, but with the eighties, a new approach to commercial music was at the fore; people were beginning to re-evaluate the relevance and purpose of the whole supergroup concept. In such regard, Lake was no different:

"Those days of forming instant supergroups are over. Most of the time, putting together big names from different groups didn't work anyway — the chemistry was usually wrong. When I left ELP, I got a lot of phone calls from people right away, asking me to join bands. I could have formed a band with a few superstar people I know. But I wanted to try this on my own to see if I could do it. If I'm a success, it will be mainly because of me. If I fail, it'll be mainly because of me. That's a different position for me to be in. So I find it interesting."

In 1980, Palmer formed a band by the name of PM with Texas blues rock guitarist John Nitzinger. Regarding his stance on ELP at that point, Palmer told *Record Mirror*; "We'd done everything. We made a perfect fusion of rock music and classical styles, and there were no more mountains to climb. We'd been together for ten years, and like marriage partners, we were beginning to get a little tired of the arrangement. Of course the press would like to have you believe that we were constantly at each other's throats and massive arguments split the band, but it just wasn't like that. We've always been good friends and that will continue. We've still got the same manager and I'd like to think that one day we can all record together again."

"We're into the eighties now," he continued. "ELP was part of a whole era and it had to be laid to rest. Today things are more jagged and basic. I wanted a band to reflect that in straight ahead rock 'n' roll. I didn't

Learning To Fly

want to form a superband with well-known musicians. I could have started some form of jazz rock band, but that would have been a cop-out. I kept very quiet about forming the new band; only a few people in the music business knew about it."

"I'm still into theatrics and I'd like to spin around on stage," he said. "We've been offered a support slot on the Average White Band tour, but I'm unsure about that. I think the band needs to develop more of an identity before we go out on the road, so I think we'll take it easy for a while... I'd like to crack Europe first. We treat music as a total art form over here. Rock 'n' roll may have come from the States, but we were largely responsible for polishing it into the force it is today. I'd like to start off by playing one-thousand-seater venues and then working up. You only learn and progress if you build up gradually. I'm not going to go out and say 'Listen to me, I'm Carl Palmer. I used to be with ELP'. I didn't want to slap my name all over the place because we're making equal contributions in the band. At the moment, I feel excited because it's like starting all over again."

And indeed, things were looking good for PM. With ELP's backlist all proving as steady sellers, Carl was able to finance his new band himself. He was also given a sponsorship deal from Seiko Watches, who had approached him due to the name of his band. Also, it comes across that the time served with ELP had gone quite a way towards informing the drummer's abilities as a businessman. Regarding the *1PM* album, which was selling well at the time, Carl said; "I make sure personally that the product is reaching the shops. That way, I can attend marketing meetings and give people hell if it isn't. That's really the only way to survive. For me, music is a total commitment from recording an album to actually making sure it gets on the shelves and getting it promoted properly. I don't go home and put my feet up once I'm out of the recording studio. If you do that, things start to slip and the rip-offs start happening. Back in the ELP days, there were occasions when some firms only paid us half the money we were owed. So when we got a cheque, we wouldn't put it in the bank until we had a company audited to make sure they were paying us the right amount."

PM made one album prior to Palmer teaming up with John Wetton and Steve Howe in early 1981. Unlike Lake, for Palmer, by this point, the aim was to form a new supergroup. Enter one Geoff Downes and then Asia was born. The band was nominated at the twenty-fifth Annual Grammy Awards for Best New Artist. Palmer was only the second artist to be nominated twice for the award (David Crosby was the first). In 1991, Palmer would leave Asia in order to reunite with Emerson and Lake. After numerous personnel changes over the years, the four founding members of

Asia, Palmer included, would get back together in 2006.

In 1981, Emerson released his solo album, *Honky*. He recorded it in The Bahamas with local musicians. It marked a strong deviation from Emerson's usual style in how it showcased material that was calypso and reggae inspired. Commercially, the album didn't go down well. Thereafter, Emerson's solo releases were few and far between. He did however, proceed to write and perform music for films. His classical style and use of orchestras made him well-suited to film work. He excelled in that field rather than aiming for the new wave dominated pop/rock market. Emerson contributed soundtrack music to a number of films including: Dario Argento's *Inferno* (1980), *Nighthawks* (1981), *Best Revenge* (1984), Lucio Fulci's *Murderock* (1984), and Michele Soavi's *The Church* (also known as *La Chiesa*) (1989). He also composed for the short-lived 1994 US animated television series, *Iron Man*.

"After the end of ELP, I just didn't feel in the frame of mind to form another band," Emerson told *Music Week* in October 1984. "I wanted to get involved in a whole new field of music. Writing music for films seemed a logical extension to what I'd been doing in Emerson, Lake and Palmer, and I felt that the Hollywood film music industry needed some new blood — it had been dominated for a long time by the same few people, names like John Williams and Henry Mancini. It is disciplined work because the film does take priority — the music has to certainly help the film, and that of course goes against all the things I had done in the past. I keep getting asked to write the music for what are really quite abysmal films, but I have to believe in the film's plot first before I'll agree to work on it."

With regards to what he would work on next, there was a chance that pretty much anything could have been on the horizon. "There have been offers from various record companies, and it is good to know that there is still a lot of interest in me," he said. "In fact, I've been having talks with Greg Lake about the possibility of working together, but there's certainly nothing imminent at the moment."

Emerson's sporadic solo releases included a Christmas album in 1988, and the album, *Changing States*. It was recorded in 1989 but it wasn't released until 1995 after a number of the songs had already been re-recorded and released as different versions on ELP's 1992 comeback album, *Black Moon*. *Changing States* features an orchestral remake of the ELP song, 'Abaddon's Bolero' — it was recorded with the London Philharmonic Orchestra. Emerson had originally written the track, 'The Church', for the 1989 Michele Soavi horror film of the same name.

Manoeuvres, Lake's second solo album, was released in July 1983. He disbanded his group not long after completing it. He didn't promote or tour for the album. He also split from the record company.

In November 1983, Palmer invited Lake to briefly join Asia as a replacement for fellow King Crimson alumnus, John Wetton. Palmer needed Lake for four scheduled concerts in Japan. Lake agreed and spent three weeks learning Asia's songs. It culminated in his performance in the Asia In Asia concert at the Nippon Budokan Hall in Tokyo. It took place on 6th December 1983 and was the first concert to be broadcast over satellite to MTV in the US. The footage was released on home video at a later date. Lake left the group after the tour on the basis that he had only joined as a favour just to help with the Japanese concerts.

Lake explained; "Carl Palmer called me up and said: 'Could you do me a favour?'. I thought he wanted to borrow a guitar or something! He told me about the MTV broadcast from Tokyo with the whole thing set up and booked, and could I do it, since they'd fallen out with Johnny (Wetton). At first I didn't want to, since Johnny is a friend of mine, but I called him up and he told me to do it. I did the show, and we discussed the possibility of making an album, but they wanted to go in a "pop" direction, which I couldn't do; it never went any further than that."

In 1985, Emerson and Lake decided that it was time to reform Emerson, Lake and Palmer to record another album. However, Palmer was already committed to Asia. As a result, Emerson and Lake proceeded to audition other drummers. They found that they had a good rapport with drummer Cozy Powell, who had excelled in his work with Rainbow and had a fantastic reputation as a very capable and heavy drummer by then.

Emerson, Lake and Powell is sometimes abbreviated to ELPowell or ELP2 as a variant on the band's original name and members. Emerson, Lake and Powell released one eponymous studio album in 1986. The debut single from the album, 'Touch And Go', peaked at number sixty on the Billboard charts on 19th July of the same year.

A number of drummers had been auditioned before Powell was. Powell had been friends with Emerson for a long time; getting in touch to invite him to audition for the band was not difficult. The band always stipulated that Cozy's surname conveniently beginning with the letter P was coincidental rather than what qualified him to drum for the band.

Powell spoke highly of what it was to work with Emerson and Lake; "I've had to work hard with them, learning a lot of the old stuff. It's not just a three-minute twelve-bar blues you have to learn. It's been interesting working out on *Tarkus*. It's opened up my musical vocabulary. They are clever pieces of music and Keith isn't exactly a three-chord wonder. He comes up with some very clever stuff, and Greg as well. I've had to learn 'Pirates', which runs for fourteen minutes. They are also playing *Pictures*

At An Exhibition, it's not three choruses, verse and fade-out. To play this stuff, you need a lot of experience and confidence. It's not beginner's music, that's for sure. It's been a real challenge and it's brought me out from being a backing drummer, which I was in Michael Schenker Group and Whitesnake. I can express myself now and play a solo as well! So I've been practising hard and I've even stopped drinking, which a lot of people can't believe. I am determined to make this successful, I'm going to give it my best shot because the band is worthy of a good crack."

Keith recalled of ELP2's early days; "I remember Cozy being in my barn in Sussex. He set up his impressive drum rig, then realised he had no drumsticks! He considered using some fallen branches from by the orchard until a local farmer drove into town to get some proper ones. They weren't the correct weight but were sufficient when he held them upside-down using the fat end. Then he'd do his drum solo and it would be like World War Three had broken out."

The band's tour began on 15th August 1986 in El Paso, Texas. Initially, sixty-five dates were set up for as far as late October. Disappointingly though, Emerson, Lake and Powell's live tour was impaired by disagreements with the management. It resulted in the band firing them. The difficulties snowballed from there and ultimately, the band broke up.

In 1988, Emerson and Palmer teamed up with Robert Berry to form the band, 3. Their album, *To The Power Of Three*, was released in 1988.

9.
Every Day I See A New Cloud Coming

Whilst Emerson was working on a film score in 1991 for former Atlantic employee Phil Carson, he brought in Lake and Palmer to assist him. Although Palmer was still working on something with Asia at the time, he left the group. With Lake back in the fold as well, ELP began rehearsals by playing 'Tarkus' "just to get back into shape". Carson signed ELP to his new label, Victory Records.

"We started playing again," said Emerson. "It was so great that we decided to make an album."

Palmer agreed that the band's long sabbatical "helped rather than hurt, because we were able to work on outside projects, and then could bring those outside experiences back into ELP. It's not as if we sat around twiddling our thumbs since we did our last album, *Love Beach*, in 1978." It wasn't long before the word got out that ELP were going to make a comeback and soon afterwards, it was confirmed with the release of *Black Moon* in May 1992. The album's title track was released as a single. The whole album remained true to ELP's original sound and didn't go for the easier option of a more commercial sound. New advances in technology expanded the scope of what was musically possible, but it was essentially the ELP sound that fans had grown to love decades ago. The album was produced by Mark Mancina (who also wrote the track, 'Burning Bridges').

Of Mancina's production, Emerson said; "It really helped to have an objective voice involved, and Mark really brought a lot to this album. For a start, he's a good keyboard player and writer himself, and he really understands ELP's background. He knows what makes this band tick and knows how to pull the best out of all of us."

Palmer said of ELP's intentions with the album, "I think what we hope to bring back into the music industry is the sound of a group. People actually playing their instruments, a real positive side of music — unlike a lot of music that came out in the eighties, which was computer-driven with a lot of button-pushing — and I think it's now time to get that identifiable sound of a band actually playing together. We were always a live band. We designed the music to be played in a live situation and then transferred it to record. Also, now with the technology that is available to us, which we didn't have in the seventies, it is a very positive time for a progressive band to come back."

On the band being back together after a break, Lake considered; "There was a thrill, and a genuine feeling that we could make a great record. I think we all heard something none of us had heard for many years. So many bands today seem to have no recognisable sound or personality. Well, we do, and we're not going to apologise for that."

Palmer enthused; "In the early seventies when we started, we never realised the chemistry that existed. We made an album every fourteen months, toured virtually every year, so time went very quickly and we just never realised what it was. Then, coming back and playing together, we thought, 'Wow! This is just like we played yesterday' — it just happened, a bit like putting on an old pair of shoes, and I think what we've grown to appreciate, individually and collectively, is the contribution we've made to this situation — not just musically, but to the ambience of the whole thing. We're older and wiser, and thus appreciate each other more."

Black Moon showcased Lake's skills as a lyricist regarding contemporary issues. He explained; "A lot of the album was written during the Gulf crisis. 'Black Moon' came when I saw the oil wells burning in Kuwait. I was watching television one day and I saw a report about all these oil fields being set alight, and this picture had the sun blacked out by all this smoke, but you could still see it and it looked like a moon, and then a black moon, and that started me thinking."

"ELP lyrics are not what someone would call normal song material," he said. "Often, the songs are not the usual relationship-based kind. I prefer to start off with an unusual image or a scene that strikes me, then work on it from there."

When asked about how his singing had changed since the earlier days of his career, Lake explained; "I only sing the songs that I truly enjoy. And with a little more reserve, like in 'Farewell To Arms' where everyone expects me to vocally explode. Wherein my voice is concerned, it is lower and deeper. Just like the emotions of a forty-five-year-old man."

The most classical-sounding piece on *Black Moon* is ELP's version

Every Day I See A New Cloud Coming

of 'Dance Of The Knights', from Prokofiev's *Romeo and Juliet*. Emerson explained; "What struck me about this particular music was the similarity between it and the way that Jimi Hendrix started 'Purple Haze'. The rhythm was so similar that I was sure I could make it work with the Prokofiev. Amazingly, you don't have to force too many changes to make it happen. It works quite naturally, the same as the shuffle rhythm works with 'Fanfare For The Common Man'."

"There's no compromise on this new album," said Palmer. "For better or for worse, no one could ever mistake *Black Moon* for anything other than ELP, and I personally approached it as if we'd never stopped making albums." Also; "We're extremely proud of our past and of our old albums, and we see *Black Moon* as a direct descendant and continuation. Of course, everything is so much more technical today than when we started, and on this album, we've used everything that was available to us, whether it was computers or MIDI, to make the best record we could — but without sacrificing any of the personal playing, technique, vocal approach, whatever, that characterises an ELP record. We've stayed true to what we always were. You won't find any rap songs on this album."

"I think the great thing about this new album is that there was never any pressure, either from the record company or from ourselves, to do anything other than ELP," said Emerson. "It's also the most mature album we've ever recorded. We just went into the studio and did what we do best." Also; "For all those fans that feel they've been starved of music that challenges and pushes, we plan to put on a hell of a show. ELP is back!"

One journalist said of the album; "From its muscular, urgent opening chords on the first title track, through an inspired and spectacular arrangement of Prokofiev's *Romeo and Juliet*, to the final heartfelt flourishes of 'Footprints In The Snow', *Black Moon* finds ELP once again at the height of its considerable power. In an era when too many bands seem to be willing slaves of fashion and uncertain of their own convictions, ELP marches confidently across today's musical landscape, unafraid of its own shadow, happy to take risks, and secure in its own image and place in history... Certainly no one could ever accuse ELP's album of sounding like anyone else. With virtuoso keyboard player Keith Emerson back at the Hammond organ and playing at the peak of his powers, the supremely balanced trio of Emerson, Lake and Palmer has crafted an alluring aural masterpiece that is directly in the traditions of such classic ELP albums as *Brain Salad Surgery* and *Tarkus*."

Another considered; "*Black Moon* marks a grand reunion of the three men who now seem to be able to better appreciate each other; being in their mid-to-late-forties might have helped. The ELP sound is unmistakable:

Greg Lake's voice, Keith Emerson's weaving of all the keyboards from the past fifteen years, the flights of Palmer who has redefined the definition of the word "drumming"."

In June 1992, *Cash Box* reviewed the album as pick of the week: "It's refreshing to know there are still a few certain groups who aren't just trying to jump on the trendy commercial bandwagon, more worried about their hair and whether or not they have the right clothes to be able to compete in the marketplace. ELP is one of the rare breed who have established themselves so solidly, they can take as much time as they have off, come back together and make an album like *Black Moon*. It's classic ELP. Keith Emerson shows off in an amazing rendition of Prokofiev's *Romeo and Juliet*. The other nine cuts are original, including one from producer Mark Mancina."

From *Billboard*: "Fourteen years after their last studio album together, original pomp-rock triumvirate of Keith Emerson, Greg Lake and Carl Palmer regroups for another go. Keyboard-heavy approach (there are three instrumental tracks here) and platitudinous lyrics are largely unaffected by the years. Outraged 'Paper Blood' and ballad 'Farewell To Arms' (which harks back to 'Lucky Man' for subject matter) are top picks for unregenerate album rockers."

From *Gavin*: "After a decade of limbo, Emerson, Lake and Palmer stage a curious comeback. *Black Moon* makes a strong pitch for the retro market dollar. While it's hard to imagine Ride and My Bloody Valentine fans hailing the return of ELP, there must be legions of Yes and Genesis fans who long for a fresh evening of classic acrobatics. Instrumental entries such as 'Changing States' recall the majesty that ELP tended to cook up on stage. I must admit, hearing Emerson's Hammond is a bit of a kick. ELP has adapted to today's technology, and it's their most viable comeback yet. Having spent a sincere amount of time listening, I found my favourites off the beaten track — more toward disc's end. Obvious airplay picks may include 'Black Moon' or 'Paper Blood'. I prefer melodic choices like 'Burning Bridges' into the acoustic piano-ed 'Close To Home', 'Better Days' and 'Footprints In The Snow'."

Chris Welch advocated that 'Footprints In The Snow' was "the final rebuke for those who see ELP solely as some sort of bombastic machine".

In August 1992, *Cash Box* reviewed the single, 'Affairs Of The Heart'; "From the recently-reformed trio's *Black Moon* album, 'Affairs Of The Heart' is an acoustic guitar, lightly percussion-pushed ballad by Greg Lake, fantasising over an encounter with an inspirational young lady in a hotel. With Keith's tasteful keyboard accompaniment, this supergroup's music clearly hasn't been affected by the years off, and this song is an indication of the ever-changing moods they continue to create."

ELP's world tour began on 24th July 1992. "Now we can't wait to get back on stage and play these songs live," said Palmer prior to the tour. "It'll be the first time in fifteen years we play live together, and if it's anything like making this record, it's going to be a very special occasion."

With such a vast choice of material to choose from by this point, he explained how it informed the band's choice of setlist; "A show has to have a certain amount of things. You've got to have stuff from the past, and the new stuff, but the show has to have highs and lows, and it's got to have the theatrical things. I think after being away for so long too, it's nice to come back and let people see us as a group. I think that's important — apart from the fact we enjoy playing as three people."

Such was the success of the tour that extra dates were added. Emerson admitted, "We certainly hadn't anticipated this sort of response to the tour — not in the UK anyway. The reaction of the audiences in America has been fantastic. Nothing seems to have changed with regards to audience reaction. We're a little different, of course. There's no room for partying after the show as we may have done in the seventies. Things like that, you've got to be aware of. We're older and wiser now, and we keep ourselves in pretty good shape."

In August 1992, a local newspaper reported under the heading of "Emerson, Lake and Palmer Revive The Good Old Days"; "More than five-thousand people invaded the Agora last night to see and relive the works of Emerson, Lake and Palmer. The fabulous progressive trio revived an entire era for an audience that was clearly devoted and ready for the reunion. It was rather cool last night on the shores of Saint Lawrence, but the fans were able to enjoy one of the rare dry nights we have had this summer... The crowd was patiently awaiting the arrival of Keith Emerson, Greg Lake and Carl Palmer, who were warmly greeted by a standing ovation. The crowd was theirs. After only a few songs, Keith Emerson, who was surrounded by analogue keyboards from the good old days, took quite a risk when he sat down at the piano to cool things down a bit. No problem. ELP's fans are there for the music and witness the works of this incredible machine, who, during the seventies, were the bearers of the British progressive flame and they surely had a lot of material to work with. With a background of ancient columns, the three musicians satisfied themselves by performing a few tracks from their new album and satisfied the nostalgic with their beacon songs. By the way and with respect to tradition, Keith Emerson added some colour to the show, which felt a little static (all three musicians remain in place most of the time) by throwing his organ all over the place. Great to see them back again."

The ELP Story - *A Time and a Place*

In September 1992, *Cash Box* reviewed a performance that took place at California's Universal Amphitheatre; "Since it has been fourteen years between gigs, 'Welcome Back, My Friends' appropriately, is the theme for Emerson, Lake and Palmer's return to the "active file" with this nationwide tour in support of their current Victory Music CD, *Black Moon*. And friends were certainly in abundance at this show, which, for the near-capacity crowd of loyal fans, unfortunately had to end. But the audience displayed enormous appreciation at simply having their heroes back. For Emerson, Lake and Palmer fans, the song selection is only part of the fun. The fascination really, is in watching these guys work. Not only do they work with a great deal of care and energy, but they also appear to be having the time of their lives. New material like 'Black Moon', 'Paper Blood' and 'Romeo And Juliet' was well-received and blended in nicely with opening standards 'Knife-Edge' and 'Tarkus' and later, 'Pirates' and the majestic *Pictures At An Exhibition*. Greg Lake's ever-stoic presence was particularly felt with beautiful solo renderings of 'From The Beginning' and 'Still... You Turn Me On'. Lake, of course, is solid on vocals, bass and guitar, but especially noteworthy are the dynamics involved between Carl Palmer and keyboard wizard Keith Emerson, who at times were rhythmically in sync note for note with remarkable split-second precision. Emerson was, and still is, an exciting and multi-dimensional showman, and certainly commands the most attention, whether playing two keyboards at a time, or a virtuoso solo piano piece, 'Closer To Home' (from *Black Moon*), or most notably during the encore performance of *West Side Story*'s 'America' when, while lying on his back with an old Hammond organ on top of him, he plays the piece backwards, that is, the left and right hands are playing exactly the opposite of what they're supposed to be."

In January 1993, ELP began another world tour. Forthcoming in his opinion, a journalist wrote for the *New York Post* in February 1993; "It was just about six months ago when Emerson, Lake and Palmer, the ageing English art-rock trio, hit the Jones Beach Theatre with all the fury of a summer breeze. When I saw I had to hear the band again at Radio City Music Hall for the first of their two-show engagement Wednesday, it shivered me to the timbers. That midsummer's night concert was so bad I punched, pounded and pulverised the band to the point that *Post* headline man Jim Pratt topped the review with 'Give ELP An H, They Need Help'! I don't know if I should be salting up my hat for lunch, or complimenting ELP for a radical musical about-face, but the RCMH performance was enjoyable. It wasn't the greatest thing since buttered toast, but it had its moments. Although the two shows had similarities, they were by no means the same. This time around, the band was a *band*. They reacted to each other as they performed; there was interplay, drama, and even some passion as they made music. The summer show came off as a series of solos strung together by a few melodies. Yes, some of the songs did trudge on and on and on. And yes, I did nod off a couple of times during the two-hour show — despite three cups of coffee I had beforehand in anticipation of a total yawner. The key was using a few programme switch-ups — like the band following a long, intricate, wandering piece with a peppy short number such as 'Honky Tonk Train' (sic), in which Emerson played a very hot boogie-woogie piano. Another excellent switch was from the awful 'Pirates' to the crowd's favourite instrumental of the evening, 'Hoedown'."

"At Jones Beach, I enjoyed the title track of ELP's new disc, *Black Moon*, and the money-is-king song, 'Paper Blood' (also off the new CD) holds true as one of the band's best songs. 'Paper Blood' has power and makes its point in less than ten minutes. Through the night, each man had a chance to shine. Lake hit his high during his solo singing 'C'est La Vie'. His vocals were smooth despite a relatively narrow range. His voice was surprisingly good after the bad, cold-start opening he made in which he actually hit a few sour notes. I found his vocals especially fine on the band's epic *Pictures At An Exhibition*. It is a deceptively simple piece, and Lake sang it with grace. Emerson, a noted keyboard noodler, was tight during most of the show and only let himself ramble out of control during the snoozer, 'Pirates'. This is a song of epic proportions that drags on in anthem-like surges. You're probably saying, 'Hey, Dan, what are you getting at?'. What I mean is, it's too long, too disjointed, too pretentious in a neoclassical kind of way. In other words, it's a dud. Emerson was at his best in the two encore songs, the anti-war number (and maybe their best-known song), 'Lucky Man' and 'Fanfare For The Common Man'. During 'Fanfare', Emerson trashed an old keyboard, as he usually does near the close of a show. This time around, he thrashed for only a couple of minutes, keeping the focus on the music rather than cheap stage antics. Palmer remains one of the hottest drummers in rock and his powerful rhythms never failed to drive the music home. I don't often enjoy overextended drum solos. But Palmer's work is not only the exception, it is exceptional. Last time I closed my ELP review saying the public should steer clear of this group. If Emerson, Lake and Palmer can maintain the level of showmanship and musicianship they displayed at RCMH, then my warning label should be peeled off."

In January 1993, upon being asked if anything had disappointed him surrounding ELP getting back together, Lake replied; "Yes, one thing: the reaction of some of the media. Radio and also MTV, to be exact. I am personally disappointed to notice the major lack of imagination from those involved in radio. Our songs are not aired under the pretext that they do not fit into the station's sound and that the listeners will not like them. It is a shame to see how little effort is being deployed. It is not healthy and I am not just talking about us. People are tired and want to hear something new and refreshing. We cannot change anything, but nevertheless we are not, and never will be, a "hit" group. We will continue to win fans through our live performances."

Whilst partway through their international tour that followed the release of *Black Moon*, ELP took the chance to re-introduce their trademark sound with the release of *Live At The Albert Hall*.

"With this new live album, we were afforded the opportunity to revisit all the older ELP material, as well as introducing our old fans to current work," said Lake. "It was very challenging and important for us to take the primitive sounds of before, and re-record them with the aid of new sonic technologies. Plus, it was quite moving to present this affair at the prestigious Royal Albert Hall. The quality of this recording far surpasses any of my initial expectations."

"We realise that you can't be away for fifteen years and expect people to pick up where you left off," he said. "But frankly, the response has been quite moving. The loyalty is marvellous, it's like a family feeling with our fans — which luckily, there are still quite a few! That's another reason for this live album. We wanted to give a little something back to all those people who have stuck with us along the way."

Additionally, the boxset, *The Return Of The Manticore* was released in 1993. Lake said; "It's a unique retrospective of the band. There are some previously unheard recordings and some new recordings as well. I've always wanted to do a studio version of *Pictures*, and we recorded that in Dolby Surround sound. *Pictures At An Exhibition* is an ideal piece of music for that kind of technology. We also recorded one track each from bands we were in prior to ELP. We did 'Hang On To A Dream' from The Nice, which Keith was in, 'Fire' from Carl's association with the Crazy World Of Arthur Brown, and there was an abbreviated version of '21st Century Schizoid Man' for me. Those were fun to do, and there's lots of other great stuff on there as well."

Things were looking good for ELP and they went straight into the studio to work on their next album. It was initially going to be called *The Best Seat In The House* — the idea came from Dolby's advertising campaign for their TVs at the time. Eventually though, it was decided that the album would be called *In The Hot Seat*. All was not well though. Victory Records were having financial problems and it resulted in ELP being put under pressure to go in a more commercial direction than they had done with *Black Moon*.

Palmer said of the *In The Hot Seat* recording sessions; "We are not totally committed to any one direction. We have about six tracks recorded and another three we are looking at. We're not dealing with any long conceptual pieces, but we do have songs which are about seven minutes. There is nothing in the twenty-minute area as of yet, but that could change tomorrow. We have some ideas we'd like to try, but it depends on how the writing comes along. We have four or five tracks recorded that are four-to-five-minutes long, but whether or not we are going to tie them together in any way really depends on how the lyrics turn out. It's too early to say."

In The Hot Seat was the first instance in which ELP covered a Bob Dylan song, 'The Man In The Long Black Coat'. Interestingly, with their previous bands, Lake had covered 'Love You Too Much' on his first solo album; and whist with The Nice, Emerson had covered 'She Belongs To Me', 'My Back Pages' and 'Country Pie'.

As had been the case on *Black Moon*, Lake's writing dealt with contemporary issues. He wrote 'Daddy' after having seen a feature on *America's Most Wanted* regarding Sarah Ann Wood who had disappeared from home and was presumed dead. He explained, "I wrote the song originally just to get it out of my system. Not intending to record it because I thought it was a very morbid thing to do. It was a very disturbing story, but what really hit me was when Robert Wood, Sarah's father, began to talk about Sarah's loss and the fact that he wanted to be close to her and he believed she wanted to be close to him."

When working on *In The Hot Seat*, Emerson was recovering from an operation that he had, had done in relation to a blockage around his radial nerve and problems with the ulna nerve in his right arm. Not only was this difficult for him physically but also, mentally; he feared that the best of his days as a musician were behind him. Emerson wasn't the only one having trouble with his hands though. Palmer had developed carpel tunnel syndrome by this point. He eventually had to have surgery for it. Famous hands indeed though — on 23rd November, ELP were inducted into the Hollywood Rock Wall on Sunset Boulevard. They put their handprints and signatures into the cement there.

The recording sessions continued into 1994. Just before *In The Hot Seat* was released in the September of that year, it was announced that ELP's tour of the US and Japan had been cancelled. Without a tour to promote the album, it wasn't even given many reviews.

On balance though, the music itself was appreciated by some critics, and indeed many fans (if only perhaps more so in later years). At the time, *Cash Box* offered a positive review; "They've remained true to their overproduced, grandiose hearts, making maybe more noise than any other band in history. Their latest record carries on the tradition made famous with such works as *Brain Salad Surgery*, *Tarkus* and *Pictures At An Exhibition*. And what other band would think to include a nearly fifteen-minute version of *Pictures At An Exhibition*, this time presented in Dolby Surround sound, just in case you missed any of the truly important intricacies the first time around. And they were important. Just listen to the music."

Years later, Emerson said of the album, "The sun has shone a little more for me in the past." Lake considered, "I didn't really like the album very much in the end."

By early 1995, ELP had nothing in the pipeline and the early discussions of whether or not to do a twenty-fifth anniversary tour were put aside. In the spring though, Emerson released *Changing States*. Meanwhile, Palmer began work on a new project with John Wetton and the guitarist Misha Calvin. The band went by the name of K2 and although they did have a little bit of interest, they ultimately didn't manage to strike up a record deal. With other irons in the fire, Palmer started to prepare to offer drum clinics (he still runs them to this very day — they include continuing professional development for fellow musicians, as well as work with schools and learners with special education needs). Lake had already started working on songs for a solo album. Towards the end of the year, ELP were in the process of trying to change record companies. Victory's back catalogue was taken on by Rhino Records.

In 1996, talks of touring with Yes had fallen through but it was announced that ELP would be touring the States and Japan as the support act for Jethro Tull. Tull's frontman Ian Anderson spoke of how ELP were "thoroughly nice people to work with". Emerson recalled, "The tour with Jethro Tull eliminated a lot of possible pressures that I anticipated after not having played on stage for such a long time and having gone through surgery, it actually gave me the confidence to go to Japan."

In June 1998, some of the original T-Bones had a reunion. There was also a reunion of The Nice not long after. All reunions consisted of sporadic live performances. August 1998 saw ELP embark on what would be their last ever tour together. They co-headlined with Deep Purple and Dream Theater. By late 1998, an ELP tour was booked for the following spring by Jim Davidson (yep, the comedian has also worked as a promoter). It fell through though; by December, ELP had split up.

Still prolific as individuals, in the same year, Emerson recorded a live album with Glenn Hughes and Marc Bonilla where they did their own version of 'Tarkus'. Emerson said that it "really cooked".

Every Day I See A New Cloud Coming

After an Asia reunion fell through in 1999, for a while, Palmer played in a band named after himself: Palmer. It featured Shaun Baxter on guitar and Dave Marks on bass. The group played ELP instrumental pieces.

10.
A Legend

As part of Ringo Starr's All-Starr Band, Lake began a tour of the US in July 2001. Consisting of twenty-eight dates, the line-up included Mott The Hoople's Ian Hunter, Supertramp's Roger Hodgson, and Howard Jones. As well as playing Ringo's material, the band played some of their own songs too. Lake's were 'Lucky Man', 'Karn Evil 9' and 'The Court Of The Crimson King'. He said; "Touring and performing with Ringo Starr was a great experience. Aside from being one of my musical heroes, Ringo was just a terrific person to be around. I absolutely fell in love with the band. They are all such wonderful people and enormously talented musicians. We were all from different styles of music but somehow there was a spiritual connection. Ringo brought the whole band together and after only ten days of rehearsal, we were performing a two-and-a-half-hour show. When bearing in mind the complexity of some of the material and the fact that it was the first time that any of us had ever played together, it was a pretty remarkable achievement. After spending nearly two months playing with Ringo, I came to see a deeper picture of just how important he was to the creative power and ultimate success of The Beatles. Not only is he a great rock drummer and a dedicated musician, but he also has an impressive sense of realism and humility. He was, I have to say, a total pro in every respect."

In January 2002, Emerson took part in a BBC Two Radio series called *Live From The Stables*, in which he played with Johnny Dankworth and Cleo Laine. In the same year, The Nice also got together to play a live show at The 100 Club on Oxford Street. Despite his initial reluctance to release a piano album, in May 2002, *Emerson Plays Emerson* was released on the EMI Classical label.

To address the continued talk and rumours regarding whether or not another ELP reunion was on the cards, Lake posted a message on his official website in August 2002. He stated; "I really do have very fond memories of some great times playing with ELP. It was an extraordinary band. However, the beauty of some things is that they happen in a particular way and at a particular moment in time and, because they cannot be easily duplicated, they become unique and special. For me, both the music of ELP and, for that matter, the music of King Crimson, fall into that category. It isn't just a question of the three guys getting back together for old times' sake. So many factors went into making those early albums as creatively successful as they were. I'm not honestly sure, even with the good will of all those concerned, if the same degree of innovative creativity could be replicated in the same way today. Onward and upward."

2003 was a busy year for Emerson. He had his own radio show; a weekly half-an-hour called *Emo's Memos*. In the July, his autobiography was published. In October 2003, The Nice did a twelve-date tour of the UK.

In the same year, Lake revealed that he was close to finishing an album of new recordings of some of his most prominent songs. It wasn't released until 2013 though. The thought that went into the project was substantial. Lake said; "I always wondered what it would be like if we could have had today's technology back in the days when these songs were originally cut."

2003 saw Palmer release his album, *Working Live — Volume 1*. It features a live recording from July 2001 of his band playing at The Robin in Bilston. In 2004, *Working Live — Volume 2* was released.

In 2005, a thirty-fifth anniversary DVD was released in celebration of ELP's career. Lake said; "There's stuff on there which I didn't even realise had been filmed. It's astonishing when you see the footage. You think, 'However did that get filmed? I never saw any cameras!'." The release of the DVD fuelled speculation regarding the prospect of another ELP reunion. By this time though, Emerson had commitments with The Nice; they had begun touring in late 2004 as the support group for the Scorpions.

The reunion didn't happen and Lake began working with The Who. He was asked by Roger Daltrey to take part in a benefit concert for the National Teenage Cancer trust. The show went so well that Lake was invited to do further sessions with the band.

Emerson, Lake and Palmer continued with their individual projects until it was announced that they would be headlining *Classic Rock*'s High Voltage Festival in July 2010 at London's Victoria Park. It was initially believed that the gig would be the only reunion, but in January 2010, it was announced that Emerson and Lake would tour the US doing a few small acoustic shows. Palmer was unable to commit due to his work with Asia. As a result, anticipation was high for the trio's reunion at the High Voltage

A Legend

Festival. Getting all three musicians on stage together was a big deal by that time, but it was certainly worth it.

Although Emerson had been keen to bring back his spinning piano for the High Voltage Festival, he wasn't allowed to on the basis that the local authority insisted the plan did not meet health and safety standards. Still though, ELP played through their old classics and it was a beautiful way to celebrate forty years of phenomenal music. However, Emerson said; "It's very unlikely that we'll ever play together again, so I think Greg, Carl and I should leave the stage on a positive note and not make the mistake of returning to sour the memory." Palmer confessed later, "It was a good time to wrap things up. I felt we weren't cutting-edge anymore. I told the others that was it for me, it's over." Four days after the High Voltage Festival, Palmer was back on tour with Asia.

In 2012, Lake went on the road with his show, Songs Of A Lifetime. Performing as a one-man band occasionally joined by guests, he played ELP songs as well as others he was fond of by other artists.

Palmer went on a world tour in 2013 with guitarist Paul Bielatowicz and bassist Simon Fitzpatrick. He then embarked on the 2014 Rhythm Of Light tour in the November of that year. He undertook an ELP Legacy tour in 2016, and again in 2017. On 2nd April 2019, it was announced that he would play with both Asia and his ELP Legacy band during The Royal Affair tour with Yes and John Lodge. Arthur Brown was announced as a guest vocalist partway through the tour.

Emerson made his conducting debut in September 2013 in Bowling Green with Orchestra Kentucky. He conducted the South Shore Symphony at his seventieth birthday tribute concert at Molloy College in Rockville Centre, New York in October 2014. The performance included the premiere of his three string quartets, as well as his version of 'Piano Concerto No.1' by Jeffrey Biegel.

On 9th January 2016, Lake was awarded an honorary degree in music and lyrics composition from Conservatorio Nicolini in Piacenza, Italy. He had spent several years writing his autobiography and it was originally going to be released in 2012. Poignantly though, it was released posthumously in June 2017.

Keith Emerson died on 11th March 2016 of a self-inflicted gunshot wound to the head. His body was found at his Santa Monica home in California. The medical examiner who carried out the autopsy ruled that Emerson had died of suicide in relation to depression associated with alcohol. Emerson's girlfriend, Mari Kawaguchi, revealed how he had become "depressed, nervous and anxious" due to having nerve damage that compromised his playing. In particular, she expressed that Emerson was worried that he wouldn't perform well at upcoming concerts in Japan; he was anxious that he would disappoint his fans.

Emerson was buried at Lancing and Sompting Cemetery in West Sussex on 1st April 2016. Palmer and Lake both issued statements on his death. Palmer said; "Keith was a gentle soul whose love for music and passion for his performance as a keyboard player will remain unmatched for many years to come." Lake said; "As sad and tragic as Keith's death is, I would not want this to be the lasting memory people take away with them. What I will always remember about Keith Emerson, was his remarkable talent as a musician and composer and his gift and passion to entertain. Music was his life, and despite some of the difficulties he encountered, I am sure that the music he created will live on forever."

Lake died later that same year on 7th December after suffering from cancer. When his manager announced the news on Twitter, he described Lake's battle with the illness as having been "long and stubborn". Many fellow musicians paid tribute, including Rick Wakeman, Steve Hackett, Ringo Starr, John Wetton, and indeed, Carl Palmer, who is of course, the last surviving member of ELP.

Endearingly, Palmer's approach to the situation is pragmatic, and one that certainly does justice to the legacy of ELP today. "The legacy is important, and I've looked after it in what I think is the most honest way. I'm out there playing the music," he said. "In my band, I didn't want to replace Greg or Keith and I didn't even want a keyboard player, but we can reproduce the sound quite closely. It shows you a different flavour and the versatility of ELP's music. It's the way to go for me and I'm enjoying it. I like the musical depth I have with my own band. It's really uplifting to play some of the ELP stuff, like *Pictures* and 'Tarkus'. It's all rewarding and I do feel that someone has to keep it going, so here I am."

Lake had told *Beat Instrumental* in January 1971; "I want someone in two-hundred years' time to pick up an ELP album and say 'Christ, that's a gas!'." Well, at the time of writing this book, some of ELP's most iconic albums are nearing their fiftieth anniversary — and some of them have exceeded that already! With complex, memorable, and simply enjoyable music on them, here's to the band's legacy and indeed, the next one-hundred-and-fifty years, for surely, the music of Emerson, Lake and Palmer is something that will easily withstand the test of time.

Discography

Studio Albums
Emerson, Lake and Palmer (1970)
Tarkus (1971)
Trilogy (1972)
Brain Salad Surgery (1973)
Works Volume 1 (1977)
Works Volume 2 (1977)
Love Beach (1978)
Black Moon (1992)
In The Hot Seat (1994)

Live Albums
Pictures At An Exhibition (1971)
Welcome Back, My Friends, To The Show That Never Ends – Ladies And Gentlemen, Emerson, Lake and Palmer (1974)
In Concert (1979)
Live At The Royal Albert Hall (1993)
Works Live (1993)
Live At The Isle Of Wight Festival (1997)
Live In Poland (1997)
King Biscuit Flower Hour – Greatest Hits Live (1997)
Then And Now (1998)
The Original Bootleg Series From The Manitcore Vaults – Volume 1 (2001)
The Original Bootleg Series From The Manitcore Vaults – Volume 2 (2001)
The Original Bootleg Series From The Manitcore Vaults – Volume 3 (2002)
The Original Bootleg Series From The Manitcore Vaults – Volume 4 (2006)
A Time And A Place (2010)
Live At Nassau Coliseum '78 (2011)
Live At The Mar Y Sol Festival '72 (2011)
Live In California '74 (2012)
Live In Montreal 1977 (2013)
Once Upon A Time – Live In South America 1997 (2015)
Live At Montreux 1997 (2015)
Masters From The Vaults (2017)
Live At Pocono International Raceway, USA, 8th July 1972 (2019)
(Emerson and Lake sans Palmer) Live From Manticore Hall 2010 (2014)

Singles
Lucky Man (1970)
Stones Of Years (1971)
Nut Rocker (1972)
From The Beginning (1972)
Jerusalem (1973)
Fanfare For The Common Man (1977)
C'est La Vie (1977)
Watching Over You (1978)
All I Want Is You (1978)

The ELP Story - *A Time and a Place*

Peter Gunn (1979)
Black Moon (1992
Affairs Of The Heart (1992)
Daddy (1994)

Emerson, Lake and Powell's Albums
Emerson, Lake and Powell (1986)
The Sprocket Sessions (2003)
Live In Concert (2003)

Emerson, Lake and Powell's Singles
Touch And Go (1986)

Keith Emerson and Carl Palmer with 3 Albums
To The Power Of Three (1988)

Keith Emerson and Carl Palmer with 3 Singles
Talkin' 'Bout (1988)

Keith Emerson with The Nice Albums
The Thoughts Of Emerlist Davjack (1967)
Ars Longa Vita Brevis (1968)
Nice (1969)
Five Bridges (1970)
Elegy (1971)

Keith Emerson with The Nice Singles
The Thoughts Of Emerlist Davjack (1967)
America (1968)
Brandenburger (1968)
She Belongs To Me (1969)
Country Pie (1970)

Keith Emerson's Solo Albums
Inferno (1980)
Nighthawks (1981)
Honky (1981)
Harmageddon (1983)
Murderock (1984)
Best Revenge (1984)
La Chiesa (The Church) (1989)
The Christmas Album (1989)
Changing States (1995)
America - The BBC Sessions (1996)
Iron Man Volume 1 (2001)
The Swedish Radio Sessions (2001)
BBC Sessions (2002)
Emerson Plays Emerson (2002)
Vivacitas Box Set (2003)
At The Movies Box Set (2005)

Discography

Off The Shelf (2006)
The Keith Emerson Band Featuring Marc Bonilla (2008)
Live At The Fillmore East – December 1969 (2009)
The Diamond Hard Blue Apples Of The Moon (2010)
Moscow Live (2011)
The Three Fates Project (2012)

Keith Emerson's Singles
Honky Tonk Train Blues (1976)

Keith Emerson's Soundtrack Albums
Inferno (1980)
Nighthawks (1981)
Best Revenge (1985)
Murderock (1984)
Harmageddon/China Free Fall (1987)
(A split album with Derek Austin. Emerson did the *Harmageddon* soundtrack whilst Austin did the *China Free Fall* soundtrack.)
La Chiesa (2002)
(Music from the 1989 horror film *The Church*, also known as *La Chiesa*. The album also contains material by Fabio Pignatelli and Goblin.)
Godzilla: Final Wars (2004)

Keith Emerson's Contributions
Back Against The Wall (2005)
('In The Flesh?' (two versions) and 'Waiting For The Worms' on the Pink Floyd tribute album.)
'Black Dog' on the Led Zeppelin tribute album *Led Box: The Ultimate Led Zeppelin Tribute* (2008)
Spinal Tap – 'Heavy Duty' on *Back From The Dead* (2009)
Boys Club – Live From California (with Glenn Hughes, Marc Bonilla) (2009)
Ayreon – 'Progressive Waves' on *The Theory Of Everything* (2013)

Greg Lake with The Shame Singles
Don't Go Away Little Girl (1967)

Greg Lake with The Shy Limbs Singles
Reputation (1968)

Greg Lake with King Crimson Albums
In The Court Of The Crimson King (1969)
In The Wake Of Poseidon (1970)
Epitaph (1997)

Greg Lake's Solo Albums
Greg Lake (1981)
Manoeuvres (1983)
King Biscuit Flower Hour Presents Greg Lake (1995)
The Greg Lake Retrospective – From The Beginning (1997)
From The Underground – The Official Bootleg (1998)

The ELP Story - *A Time and a Place*

Live (2000)
Nuclear Attack (2002)
From The Underground 2 – Deeper Into The Mine – An Official Greg Lake Bootleg (2003)
Songs Of A Lifetime (2013)
(With Geoff Downes 1989-1990) Ride The Tiger (2015)
Live In Piacenza 2012 (2017)

Greg Lake's Solo Singles
I Believe In Father Christmas (1975)

Carl Palmer with The Craig Singles
I Must Be Mad (1966)

Carl Palmer with Chris Farlowe and The Thunderbirds Singles
Movin' (1967)

Carl Palmer with Atomic Rooster Albums
Atomic Rooster (1970)

Carl Palmer with PM Albums
1PM (1980)

Carl Palmer with PM Singles
Dynamite (1980)

Carl Palmer with Quango Albums
Live In The Hood (2000)

Carl Palmer with Asia Albums
Asia (1982)
Alpha (1983)
Astra (1985)
Then And Now (1980)
Live In Moscow (1991)
Live In Nottingham (1991)
Aqua (1992)
Alive In Hallowed Halls (2001)
Quadra (2002)
Fantasia – Live In Tokyo (2007)
Phoenix (2008)
Under The Bridge – Live In San Francisco (2008)
Spirit Of The Night – Live In Cambridge (2009)
Omega (2010)
Resonance – The Omega Tour (2012)
XXX (2012)
Gravitas (2014)

Carl Palmer with Asia Singles
Heat Of The Moment (1982)

Discography

Here Comes The Feeling (1982)
Only Time Will Tell (1982)
Sole Survivor (1982)
Time Again (1982)
Wildest Dreams (1982)
Don't Cry (1983)
True Colours (1983)
The Heat Goes On (1983)
Daylight (1983)
The Smile Has Left Your Eyes (1983)
Go (1985)
Wishing (1986)
Too Late (1986)
Days Like These (1990)
Prayin' 4 A Miracle (1990)
Face On The Bridge (2012)

Carl Palmer's Solo Albums
Carl Palmer Band – Working Live – Volume 1 (2003)
Carl Palmer Band – Working Live – Volume 2 (2004)
Carl Palmer Band – Working Live – Volume 3 (2010)

Carl Palmer's ELP Legacy Albums
Live In The USA (2016)
Pictures At An Exhibition – A Tribute To Keith Emerson (2016)
Live (2018)

The ELP Story - *A Time and a Place*

Tour Dates

For avoidance of doubt, all date formats are day-month-year.

23/8/1970   Guildhall, Plymouth, England
29/8/1970   Isle of Wight Music Festival, Afton Down, England
4/9/1970   Open-Air Love and Peace Festival, Island of Fehmarn, Germany
(ELP were originally scheduled, but did not perform)
19/9/1970   Winter Gardens, Malvern, England
21/9/1970   Civic Hall, Wolverhampton, England
24/9/1970   Town Hall, Watford, England
25/9/1970   City Hall, Hull, England
26/9/1970   Starlight Rooms, Boston, England
27/9/1970   De Montfort Hall, Leicester, England
28/9/1970   Guildhall, Portsmouth, England
1/10/1970   Town Hall, Leeds, England
4/10/1970   City Hall, Newcastle, England
7/10/1970   The Dome, Brighton, England
9/10/1970   Greens Playhouse, Glasgow, Scotland
11/10/1970   Caird Hall, Dundee, Scotland
16/10/1970   Northeast London Polytechnic, London, England
17/10/1970   Brunel University, Uxbridge, England
19/10/1970   Colston Hall, Bristol, England
20/10/1970   Winter Gardens, Bournemouth, England
21/10/1970   Town Hall, Birmingham, England
25/10/1970   Fairfield Hall, Croydon, England
26/10/1970   Royal Festival Hall, London, England
27/10/1970   City (Oval) Hall, Sheffield, England
28/10/1970   St George's Main Hall, Liverpool, England (cancelled)
22/11/1970   St George's Main Hall, Liverpool, England
28/11/1970   Kongresshalle, Frankfurt, Germany
29/11/1970   Cirkus Khrone, Munich, Germany
30/11/1970   ?, Nuremberg, Germany
1/12/1970   Konzerthaus, Vienna, Austria
2/12/1970   Sporthalle, Boblingen, Germany
4/12/1970   Limmathaus, Zurich, Switzerland
7/12/1970   Free Trade Hall, Manchester, England
8/12/1970   St George's Hall, Bradford, England
9/12/1970   Lyceum Strand, London, England
12/12/1970   Leeds University, Leeds, England
13/12/1970   Kinetic Circus, Birmingham, England

4/2/1971   Guildhall, Southampton, England
4/3/1971   ABC, Stockton, England
5/3/1971   ABC, Hull, England
6/3/1971   ABC, Lincoln, England
7/3/1971   The Regal, Cambridge, England
10/3/1971   Capitol, Cardiff, Wales
12/3/1971   ABC, Plymouth, England
14/3/1971   Civic Hall, Wolverhampton, England
17/3/1971   Odeon, Cheltenham, England
18/3/1971   Big Apple, Brighton, England
21/3/1971   ABC, Blackpool, England
22/3/1971   Free Trade Hall, Manchester, England
23/3/1971   St George's Hall, Bradford, England
24/3/1971   City (Oval) Hall, Sheffield, England

Tour Dates

26/3/1971	City Hall, Newcastle, England (*Pictures At An Exhibition* recording)
28/3/1971	Odeon Theatre, Lewisham, England
29/3/1971	Winter Gardens, Margate, England
30/3/1971	Guildhall, Portsmouth, England
1/4/1971	ABC, Wigan, England
2/4/1971	Green's Playhouse, Glasgow, Scotland
3/4/1971	Caird Hall, Dundee, Scotland
6/4/1971	Winter Gardens, Bournemouth, England
7/4/1971	De Monfort Hall, Leicester, England
8/4/1971	St George's Hall, Liverpool, England
9/4/1971	Odeon Theatre, Birmingham, England
21/4/1971	Theil College, Greenville, PA, USA
23/4/1971	Eastown Theatre, Detroit, MI, USA
24/4/1971	Eastown Theatre, Detroit, MI, USA
25/4/1971	The Spectrum, Philadelphia, PA, USA
27/4/1971	Stanley Theatre, Pittsburgh, PA, USA
28/4/1971	Student Union Centre, Fairleigh Dickinson University, Teaneck, NJ, USA
30/4/1971	Fillmore East, New York, NY, USA (early show)
30/4/1971	Fillmore East, New York, NY, USA (late show)
1/5/1971	Fillmore East, New York, NY, USA
2/5/1971	Painters Mill Music Theatre, Owings Mills, MD, USA
3/5/1971	Shea Theatre, Buffalo, NY, USA
6/5/1971	Loews State Theatre, Providence, RI, USA
7/5/1971	Viking Memorial Hall, Upsala College East Orange, NJ, USA
11/5/1971	Guthrie Theatre, Minneapolis, MN, USA
12/5/1971	Milwaukee Arena, Milwaukee, WI, USA
14/5/1971	Public Hall, Cleveland, OH, USA
15/5/1971	Community War Memorial, Rochester, NY, USA
16/5/1971	Alexandria Roller Rink, Alexandria, VA, USA
19/5/1971	Kiel Opera House, St Louis, MO, USA
21/5/1971	Wabash College Gymnasium, Crawfordsville, IN ,USA
22/5/1971	Cincinnati Gardens, Cincinnati, OH, USA
23/5/1971	Memorial Gym, Kent State University, Kent, OH, USA
24/5/1971	Ohio Theatre, Columbus, OH, USA
26/5/1971	Carnegie Hall, New York, NY, USA
27/5/1971	Hatch Memorial Shell, Boston, MA, USA (free concert, with Edgar Winter's White Trash)
28/5/1971	Convention Centre, Wildwood, NJ, USA
30/5/1971	Bucknell University, Lewisburg, PA, USA
2/6/1971	Schwarzwaldhalle, Karlsrhue, Germany (rescheduled to 17/6)
5/6/1971	Sporthaus, Zoffingen, Switzerland
6/6/1971	?, Zurich, Switzerland
7/6/1971	Konzerthaus, Vienna, Austria
9/6/1971	Circus Krone, Munich, Germany
10/6/1971	Stadthalle, Offenbach, Germany
11/6/1971	Meistersingerhalle, Nuremberg, Germany
12/6/1971	Concertgebouw, Amsterdam, Holland
13/6/1971	Phillipshalle, Dusseldorf, Germany
14/6/1971	Weser-Ems Halle, Oldenburg, Germany
15/6/1971	Stadthalle, Offenbach, Germany
16/6/1971	Musikhalle, Hamburg, Germany
17/6/1971	Schwarzwaldhalle, Karlsrhue, Germany
20/6/1971	Royal Theatre Drury Lane, London, England
17/7/1971	Sports Arena, San Diego, CA, USA
18/7/1971	Berkeley Community Theatre, Berkeley, CA, USA
19/7/1971	Hollywood Bowl, Los Angeles, CA, USA
23/7/1971	Agrodome, Vancouver, BC, Canada
24/7/1971	Paramount Theatre, Seattle, WA, USA
25/7/1971	Paramount Theatre, Portland, OR, USA
30/7/1971	Music Hall, Houston, TX, USA

The ELP Story - *A Time and a Place*

31/7/1971	Municipal Auditorium, San Antonio, TX, USA
4/8/1971	Municipal Auditorium, Atlanta, GA, USA
6/8/1971	Pirates World, Dania, FL, USA
7/8/1971	Pirates World, Dania, FL, USA
9/8/1971	Charlotte Coliseum, Charlotte, NC, USA
10/8/1971	The Dome, Virginia Beach, VA, USA
12/8/1971	Stanley Park, Toronto, ON, Canada
13/8/1971	Place De Nations, Montreal, QC, Canada
14/8/1971	Convention Hall, Asbury Park, NJ, USA (early show)
14/8/1971	Convention Hall, Asbury Park, NJ, USA (late show)
15/8/1971	Convention Hall, Wildwood, NJ, USA
18/8/1971	Onondaga County War Memorial, Syracuse, NY, USA
19/8/1971	Peace Bridge Centre, Buffalo, NY, USA
20/8/1971	Hara Arena, Dayton, OH, USA
21/8/1971	Auditorium Theatre, Chicago, IL, USA
22/8/1971	Syria Mosque, Pittsburgh, PA, USA
24/8/1971	Wonderland Gardens, London, ON, Canada
25/8/1971	National Arts Centre, Ottawa, ON, Canada
26/8/1971	Boston Common, Boston, MA, USA
28/8/1971	Public Auditorium, Cleveland, OH, USA
30/8/1971	Bushnell Memorial Hall, Hartford, CT, USA
31/8/1971	Alexandria Roller Rink, Alexandria, VA, USA
1/9/1971	Gaelic Park, New York, NY, USA
13/11/1971	The Spectrum, Philadelphia, PA, USA
14/11/1971	Auditorium Theatre, Chicago, IL, USA
15/11/1971	Eastown Theatre, Detroit, MI, USA
16/11/1971	Eastown Theatre, Detroit, MI, USA
17/11/1971	Eastown Theatre, Detroit, MI, USA
19/11/1971	Hirsch Memorial Coliseum, Shreveport, LA, USA
20/11/1971	The Warehouse, New Orleans, LA, USA
22/11/1971	Municipal Auditorium, Atlanta, GA, USA
25/11/1971	Madison Square Garden, New York, NY, USA
26/11/1971	Civic Arena, Pittsburgh, PA, USA
27/11/1971	Farm Show Arena, Harrisburg, PA, USA
28/11/1971	Richmond Arena, Richmond, VA, USA
29/11/1971	Lyric Theatre, Baltimore, MD, USA
30/11/1971	Music Hall, Boston, MA, USA
8/12/1971	City Hall, Newcastle, England (early show)
8/12/1971	City Hall, Newcastle, England (late show)
9/12/1971	City (Oval) Hall, Sheffield, England
10/12/1971	Free Trade Hall, Manchester, England (early show)
10/12/1971	Free Trade Hall, Manchester, England (late show)
11/12/1971	Odeon Theatre, Birmingham, England (early show)
11/12/1971	Odeon Theatre, Birmingham, England (late show)
12/12/1971	Capitol, Cardiff, Wales
13/12/1971	London Pavilion, London, England
14/12/1971	London Pavilion, London, England (early show)
14/12/1971	London Pavilion, London, England (late show)
15/12/1971	London Pavilion, London, England
17/12/1971	Caird Hall, Dundee, Scotland
18/12/1971	Empire, Edinburgh, Scotland
19/12/1971	Green's Playhouse, Glasgow, Scotland (early show)
19/12/1971	Green's Playhouse, Glasgow, Scotland (late show)
21/3/1972	Denver Coliseum, Denver, CO, USA
22/3/1972	Long Beach Arena, Long Beach, CA, USA
23/3/1972	Civic Auditorium, Santa Monica, CA, USA (early show)
23/3/1972	Civic Auditorium, Santa Monica, CA, USA (late show)
24/3/1972	Winterland Arena, San Francisco, CA, USA

Tour Dates

25/3/1972	Winterland Arena, San Francisco, CA, USA
26/3/1972	St Louis Arena, St Louis, MO, USA
28/3/1972	Municipal Auditorium Atlanta, GA, USA
29/3/1972	?, Orlando, FL, USA (unconfirmed)
30/3/1972	Bayfront Centre Arena, St Petersburg, FL, USA
31/3/1972	Convention Hall, Miami, FL, USA
1/4/1972	Jacksonville Coliseum, Jacksonville, FL, USA
2/4/1972	Mar Y Sol Festival, San Juan, PR, USA
4/4/1972	New Haven Arena, New Haven, CT, USA (rescheduled from 9/3)
5/4/1972	Music Hall, Boston, MA, USA
7/4/1972	Utica Memorial Auditorium, Utica, NY, USA
8/4/1972	Memorial Auditorium, Buffalo, NY, USA
9/4/1972	College of Wooster Gym, Wooster, OH, USA
10/4/1972	Academy of Music, New York, NY, USA (early show)
10/4/1972	Academy of Music, New York, NY, USA (late show)
11/4/1972	Academy of Music, New York, NY, USA (early show)
11/4/1972	Academy of Music, New York, NY, USA (late show)
12/4/1972	Bucknell University, Lewisburg, PA, USA
13/4/1972	Mayser Centre, Franklin and Marshall College, Lancaster, PA, USA
14/4/1972	Sports Arena, Hershey, PA, USA
15/4/1972	The Spectrum, Philadelphia, PA, USA
17/4/1972	Cobo Arena, Detroit, MI, USA
18/4/1972	Hara Arena, Dayton, OH, USA
19/4/1972	Arie Crown Theatre, Chicago, IL, USA (early and late shows, rescheduled from 17/3)
20/4/1972	Ohio University Convocation Centre, Athens, OH, USA
21/4/1972	Convention Centre, Louisville, KY, USA
22/4/1972	Will Rogers Memorial Coliseum, Fort Worth, TX, USA
23/4/1972	Hofheinz Pavilion, Houston, TX, USA
25/4/1972	University of Cincinnati, Cincinnati, OH, USA (cancelled)
26/4/1972	Academy of Music, New York, NY, USA (cancelled)
27/4/1972	Theil College, Greenville, PA, USA (cancelled)
28/4/1972	Montreal Forum, Montreal, QC, Canada (cancelled)
29/4/1972	Colisèe, Quebec City, QC, Canada (cancelled)
4/6/1972	Grugahalle, Essen, Germany
5/6/1972	Munsterlandhalle, Munster, Germany
6/6/1972	Deutchlandhalle, Berlin, Germany
7/6/1972	Musikhalle, Hamburg, Germany
8/6/1972	Falkoner Theatre, Copenhagen, Denmark
10/6/1972	Festhalle, Frankfurt, Germany
11/6/1972	Meistersingerhalle, Nurnberg, Germany
12/6/1972	Stadthalle, Vienna, Austria
14/6/1972	Stadio Comunale, Bologna, Italy (rescheduled to 25/6)
15/6/1972	Palazzo Dello Sport, Genova, Italy
17/6/1972	Crystal Palace, London, England (cancelled)
19/6/1972	Olympia Theatre, Paris, France
24/6/1972	Mehrzweckhalle, Wetzikon, Switzerland
25/6/1972	Stadio Comunale, Bologna, Italy
26/6/1972	Palazzo Dello Sport, Rome, Italy
8/7/1972	Pocono International Raceway, Long Pond, PA, USA (Concert 10)
22/7/1972	Korakuen Stadium, Tokyo, Japan
24/7/1972	Korakuen Stadium, Tokyo, Japan
27/7/1972	Civic Auditorium, San Francisco, CA, USA
28/7/1972	Long Beach Arena, Long Beach, CA, USA
29/7/1972	Seattle Centre Arena, Seattle, WA, USA
1/8/1972	Municipal Auditorium, Kansas City, MO, USA
3/8/1972	Charlotte Coliseum, Charlotte, NC, USA
4/8/1972	Municipal Auditorium, Birmingham, AL, USA
5/8/1972	Auditorium North Hall, Memphis, TN ,USA
6/8/1972	The Warehouse, New Orleans, LA, USA

The ELP Story - *A Time and a Place*

7/8/1972   Municipal Auditorium, Mobile, AL, USA
9/8/1972   Mississippi River Festival, Edwardsville, IL, USA
10/8/1972   The Armory, Minneapolis, MN, USA
11/8/1972   Milwaukee Arena, Milwuakee, WI, USA
12/8/1972   Civic Arena, Pittsburgh, PA, USA
13/8/1972   Saratoga Performing Arts Centre, Saratoga Springs, NY, USA
15/8/1972   Montreal Forum, Montreal, QC, Canada
16/8/1972   Colisée de Québec, Quebec City, QC, Canada
17/8/1972   Arie Crown Theatre, Chicago, IL, USA (uncertain)
18/8/1972   War Memorial Auditorium, Rochester, NY, USA
19/8/1972   Convention Hall, Asbury Park, NJ, USA (early show)
19/8/1972   Convention Hall, Asbury Park, NJ, USA (late show)
20/8/1972   Merriweather Post Pavilion, Columbia, MD, USA
6/9/1972   ?, Brandside, England
30/9/1972   Kennington Cricket Oval, London, England
10/11/1972   Winter Gardens, Bournemouth, England
11/11/1972   Gaumont Theatre, Southampton, England
12/11/1972   Top Rank Suite, Cardiff, Wales (postponed)
13/11/1972   Free Trade Hall, Manchester, England
14/11/1972   Hardrock Concert Theatre, Manchester, England
15/11/1972   St George's Hall, Bradford, England
16/11/1972   Odeon Theatre, Newcastle, England (cancelled)
17/11/1972   Green's Playhouse, Glasgow, Scotland (early show)
17/11/1972   Green's Playhouse, Glasgow, Scotland (late show)
18/11/1972   Guildhall, Preston, England
19/11/1972   Trentham Gardens, Stoke, England
21/11/1972   De Montfort Hall, Leicester, England
22/11/1972   Top Rank Suite, Liverpool, England
23/11/1972   Capitol, Cardiff, Wales (early show)
23/11/1972   Capitol, Cardiff, Wales (late show)
24/11/1972   Odeon Theatre, Birmingham, England (early show)
24/11/1972   Odeon Theatre, Birmingham, England (late show)
25/11/1972   City Hall, Sheffield, England
26/11/1972   Hammersmith Odeon, London, England (early show)
26/11/1972   Hammersmith Odeon, London, England (late show)
27/11/1972   The Dome, Brighton, England
29/11/1972   Odeon, Newcastle, England (early show)
29/11/1972   Odeon, Newcastle, England (late show)
1/12/1972   Caird Hall, Dundee, Scotland

30/3/1973   Ostseehalle, Kiel, Germany
31/3/1973   Phillipshalle, Dusseldorf, Germany
1/4/1973   Forest Nationale, Brussels, Belgium
3/4/1973   Saint Ouen, Paris, France
4/4/1973   Les Arenes, Poitiers, France
5/4/1973   Palais De Sport, Caen, France (cancelled)
6/4/1973   Palais De Sport, Lille, France (cancelled)
7/4/1973   Palais Des Exposition, Nancy, France (cancelled)
8/4/1973   Palais Des Sport, Lyon, France (cancelled)
10/4/1973   Friedrich Eberthalle, Ludwigshafen, Germany
11/4/1973   Friedrich Eberthalle, Ludwigshafen, Germany
12/4/1973   Stadthalle, Freiburg, Germany
13/4/1973   Sporthalle, Koln, Germany
15/4/1973   Hallenstadion, Zurich, Switzerland
16/4/1973   Ernst-Merck Halle, Hamburg, Germany
17/4/1973   Brondby Hall, Copenhagen, Denmark
18/4/1973   Scandinavium, Gothenburg, Sweden
21/4/1973   Oude Rai, Amsterdam, Holland

Tour Dates

22/4/1973	Grosse Westfalen Halle, Dortmund, Germany
23/4/1973	Munsterlandhalle, Munster, Germany
24/4/1973	Olympiahalle, Munich, Germany
25/4/1973	Konzerthaus, Vienna, Austria
26/4/1973	Konzerthaus, Vienna, Austria
28/4/1973	Velodromo Vigorelli, Milan, Italy (postponed, Greg ill)
29/4/1973	Ponte Sant'Ambrogio, Modena, Italy (cancelled, Greg ill)
30/4/1973	Stadio Comunale, Bologna, Italy (postponed, Greg ill)
2/5/1973	Stadio Flaminio, Rome, Italy
3/5/1973	Stadio Comunale, Bologna, Italy
4/5/1973	Velodromo Vigorelli, Milan, Italy
14/11/1973	Jai-Alai Fronton, Miami, FL, USA
15/11/1973	Jai-Alai Fronton, Miami, FL, USA
16/11/1973	Veterans Memorial Coliseum, Jacksonville, FL, USA (uncertain)
17/11/1973	West Palm Beach Auditorium, West Palm Beach, FL, USA
18/11/1973	Curtis Hixon Hall, Tampa, FL, USA
19/11/1973	Municipal Auditorium, Atlanta, GA, USA (uncertain)
20/11/1973	Civic Centre, Roanoke, VA, USA (cancelled due to stage problems)
21/11/1973	Convention Centre, Louisville, KY, USA
22/11/1973	Cincinnati Gardens, Cincinnati, OH, USA
23/11/1973	Civic Centre, Charleston, WV, USA
24/11/1973	State Fairgrounds Coliseum, Indianapolis, IN, USA
25/11/1973	Municipal Auditorium, Nashville, TN, USA
26/11/1973	University of Illinois Assembly Hall, Champaign, IL, USA
28/11/1973	State Fairgrounds Arena, Oklahoma City, OK, USA
30/11/1973	Veterans Memorial Auditorium, Des Moines, IA, USA
1/12/1973	Metropolitan Sports Centre, Minneapolis, MN, USA
2/12/1973	International Amphitheatre, Chicago, IL, USA
3/12/1973	International Amphitheatre, Chicago, IL, USA
4/12/1973	Cobo Arena, Detroit, MI, USA
5/12/1973	Cobo Arena, Detroit, MI, USA
7/12/1973	Maple Leaf Gardens, Toronto, ON, Canada
8/12/1973	Barton Hall, Cornell University, Ithaca, NY, USA (cancelled)
9/12/1973	Montreal Forum, Montreal, QC, Canada
10/12/1973	Boston Garden, Boston, MA, USA
11/12/1973	The Spectrum, Philadelphia, PA, USA
13/12/1973	Nassau Coliseum, Uniondale, NY, USA
14/12/1973	Veterans Memorial Coliseum, New Haven, CT, USA
15/12/1973	Civic Centre, Baltimore, MD, USA
17/12/1973	Madison Square Garden, New York, NY, USA
18/12/1973	Madison Square Garden, New York, NY, USA
24/1/1974	The Omni, Atlanta, GA, USA
25/1/1974	Memorial Coliseum, Tuscaloosa, AL, USA
26/1/1974	Barton Coliseum, Little Rock, AR, USA
28/1/1974	Denver Coliseum, Denver, CO, USA
30/1/1974	Salt Palace, Salt Lake City, UT, USA
1/2/1974	Convention Centre, Anaheim, CA, USA
2/2/1974	Convention Centre, Anaheim, CA, USA
3/2/1974	Long Beach Arena, Long Beach, CA, USA
9/2/1974	Swing Auditorium, San Bernardino, CA, USA
11/2/1974	Seattle Centre Arena, Seattle, WA, USA
12/2/1974	Spokane Coliseum, Spokane, WA, USA
13/2/1974	Memorial Coliseum, Portland, OR, USA
14/2/1974	PNE Coliseum, Vancouver, BC, Canada
15/2/1974	WSU Performing Arts Coliseum, Pullman, WA, USA
17/2/1974	Civic Auditorium, San Francisco, CA, USA
18/2/1974	Civic Auditorium, San Francisco, CA, USA (unconfirmed)

The ELP Story - *A Time and a Place*

20/2/1974   Selland Arena, Fresno, CA, USA
21/2/1974   Sports Arena, San Diego, CA, USA
22/2/1974   Community Centre Arena, Tuscon, AZ, USA
24/2/1974   University of New Mexico Arena, Albuquerque, NM, USA
26/2/1974   Convention Centre (Hemisfair) Arena, San Antonio, TX, USA
27/2/1974   Memorial Auditorium, Dallas, TX, USA
28/2/1974   Sam Houston Coliseum, Houston, TX, USA
1/3/1974   Assembly Centre, Louisiana State University, Baton Rouge, LA, USA
3/3/1974   Municipal Auditorium, New Orleans, LA, USA (unconfirmed)
28/3/1974   Kiel Auditorium Convention Hall, St Louis, MO, USA
29/3/1974   Henry Levitt Arena, Wichita, KS, USA
31/3/1974   Mid-South Coliseum, Memphis, TN, USA
2/4/1974   Assembly Centre, Tulsa, OK, USA
6/4/1974   Ontario Motor Speedway, Ontario, CA, USA (California Jam)
18/4/1974   Wembley Empire Pool, London, England
19/4/1974   Wembley Empire Pool, London, England
20/4/1974   Wembley Empire Pool, London, England
21/4/1974   Wembley Empire Pool, London, England
23/4/1974   Trentham Gardens, Stoke, England
29/4/1974   Empire, Liverpool, England
30/4/1974   Empire, Liverpool, England
1/5/1974   Empire, Liverpool, England
7/5/1974   Palacio Municipal De Deportes, Barcelona, Spain
8/5/1974   Palacio Municipal De Deportes, Barcelona, Spain
11/5/1974   Hallenstadion, Zurich, Switzerland
13/5/1974   Messehalle, Sindelfingen, Germany
14/5/1974   Olympiahalle, Innsbruck, Austria
16/5/1974   Bundesstadion Liebenau, Graz, Austria
17/5/1974   Stadthalle, Vienna, Austria
18/5/1974   Olympiahalle, Munich, Germany
19/5/1974   Olympiahalle, Munich, Germany
20/5/1974   Mehrzweckhalle, Wetzikon, Switzerland (cancelled)
21/5/1974   Eisstadion, Mannheim, Germany
23/5/1974   Philipshalle, Dusseldorf, Germany
24/5/1974   Philipshalle, Dusseldorf, Germany
25/5/1974   Ahoy Hall, Rotterdam, Holland
26/5/1974   Forest National, Brussels, Belgium
27/5/1974   Palais des Sports, Paris, France
28/5/1974   Palais des Sports, Paris, France
31/5/1974   Festhalle, Frankfurt, Germany
1/6/1974   Festhalle, Frankfurt, Germany
2/6/1974   Ernst-Merck Halle (uncertain), Hamburg, Germany
26/7/1974   Rich Stadium, Buffalo, NY, USA (Summerfest)
28/7/1974   Yale Bowl, New Haven, CT, USA
29/7/1974   Civic Centre, Providence, RI, USA
30/7/1974   Cape Cod Coliseum, South Yarmouth, MA, USA
1/8/1974   Capital Centre, Landover, MD, USA
2/8/1974   Civic Arena, Pittsburgh, PA, USA
4/8/1974   Cleveland Stadium, Cleveland, OH, USA
6/8/1974   Richmond Coliseum, Richmond, VA, USA
7/8/1974   The Scope, Norfolk, VA, USA
10/8/1974   Charlotte Motor Speedway, Charlotte, NC, USA (August Jam)
12/8/1974   Civic Centre, Savannah, GA, USA
13/8/1974   Civic Coliseum, Knoxville, TN ,USA
14/8/1974   Hara Arena, Dayton, OH, USA
15/8/1974   Hersheypark Arena, Hershey, PA, USA
17/8/1974   Roosevelt Stadium, Jersey City, NJ, USA
(freak storm during show causes damage and rescheduling to 20/8)
18/8/1974   Saratoga Performing Arts Centre, Saratoga Springs, NY, USA

Tour Dates

(cancelled due to damaged equipment)
20/8/1974   Roosevelt Stadium, Jersey City, NJ, USA
21/8/1974   The Spectrum, Philadelphia, PA, USA

24/5/1977   Freedom Hall, Louisville, KY, USA (with orchestra)
25/5/1977   Freedom Hall, Louisville, KY, USA (with orchestra)
26/5/1977   Municipal Auditorium, Nashville, TN, USA (with orchestra)
28/5/1977   Riverfront Coliseum, Cincinnati, OH, USA (postponed)
29/5/1977   Riverfront Coliseum, Cincinnati, OH, USA (with orchestra)
31/5/1977   Cobo Arena, Detroit, MI, USA (with orchestra)
1/6/1977   Cobo Arena, Detroit, MI, USA (with orchestra)
4/6/1977   Soldier Field, Chicago, IL, USA (with orchestra)
5/6/1977   Milwaukee Arena, Milwaukee, WI, USA (with orchestra)
7/6/1977   Market Square Arena, Indianapolis, IN, USA (with orchestra)
9/6/1977   Dane County Coliseum, Madison, WI, USA (with orchestra)
11/6/1977   Civic Centre Arena, St Paul, MN, USA (with orchestra)
12/6/1977   Veterans Memorial Auditorium, Des Moines, IA, USA (with orchestra)
(orchestra dropped thereafter, apart from Madison Square Garden and Olympic Stadium shows)
14/6/1977   Hulman Civic University Centre, Terre Haute, IN, USA (cancelled)
16/6/1977   Allen County War Memorial Coliseum, Fort Wayne, IN, USA
18/6/1977   Civic Arena, Pittsburgh, PA, USA (moved from Three Rivers Stadium)
20/6/1977   The Spectrum, Philadelphia, PA, USA
21/6/1977   The Spectrum, Philadelphia, PA, USA
23/6/1977   The Omni, Atlanta, GA, USA
25/6/1977   Birmingham-Jefferson Civic Centre, Birmingham, AL, USA
27/6/1977   Civic Coliseum, Knoxville, TN, USA
28/6/1977   Greensboro Coliseum, Greensboro, NC, USA
29/6/1977   Charlotte Coliseum, Charlotte, NC, USA
30/6/1977   Carolina Coliseum, Columbia, SC, USA
2/7/1977   Tampa Stadium, Tampa, FL, USA (cancelled)
2/7/1977   The Scope Convention Hall, Norfolk, VA, USA
3/7/1977   Civic Centre, Baltimore, MD, USA
4/7/1977   Civic Centre, Charleston, WV, USA
7/7/1977   Madison Square Garden, New York, NY, USA (with orchestra)
8/7/1977   Madison Square Garden, New York, NY, USA (with orchestra)
9/7/1977   Madison Square Garden, New York, NY, USA (with orchestra)
10/7/1977   Civic Centre, Hartford, CT, USA
12/7/1977   Boston Garden, Boston, MA, USA
13/7/1977   Civic Centre, Augusta, ME, USA
14/7/1977   Civic Centre, Providence, RI, USA
16/7/1977   War Memorial Auditorium, Rochester, NY, USA
17/7/1977   Broome County Arena, Binghamton, NY, USA
19/7/1977   Richfield Coliseum, Richfield, OH, USA
20/7/1977   Onondaga County War Memorial Auditorium, Syracuse, NY, USA
22/7/1977   Cobo Arena, Detroit, MI, USA
24/7/1977   CNE Stadium, Toronto, ON, Canada
27/7/1977   The Corral, Calgary, AB, Canada
30/7/1977   Pacific Coliseum, Vancouver, BC, Canada
31/7/1977   Seattle Centre Coliseum, Seattle, WA, USA
2/8/1977   Memorial Coliseum, Portland, OR, USA
4/8/1977   Cow Palace, San Francisco, CA, USA
5/8/1977   Selland Arena, Fresno, CA, USA
6/8/1977   Oakland Coliseum Arena, Oakland, CA, USA
9/8/1977   Veterans Memorial Coliseum, Phoenix, AZ, USA
10/8/1977   Sports Arena, San Diego, CA, USA
11/8/1977   Long Beach Arena, Long Beach, CA, USA
12/8/1977   Long Beach Arena, Long Beach, CA, USA
13/8/1977   Swing Auditorium, San Bernardino, CA, USA

The ELP Story - *A Time and a Place*

14/8/1977	Long Beach Arena, Long Beach, CA, USA
15/8/1977	Aladdin Theatre, Las Vegas, NV, USA
16/8/1977	Aladdin Theatre, Las Vegas, NV, USA
17/8/1977	Salt Palace, Salt Lake City, UT, USA
19/8/1977	McNichols Arena, Denver, CO, USA
20/8/1977	Memorial Auditorium, Dallas, TX, USA
21/8/1977	Assembly Centre, Tulsa, OK, USA
22/8/1977	Municipal Auditorium, Kansas City, MO, USA
23/8/1977	Kiel Auditorium, St Louis, MO, USA
26/8/1977	Olympic Stadium, Montreal, QC, Canada (with orchestra)
12/9/1977	?, Edinburgh, Scotland*
13/9/1977	?, Edinburgh, Scotland*
14/10/1977	Wings Stadium, Kalamazoo, MI, USA
15/10/1977	Convocation Centre, Ohio University, Athens, OH, USA
17/10/1977	Madison Square Garden, New York, NY, USA
18/10/1977	Hersheypark Arena, Hershey, PA, USA
19/10/1977	Sports Arena, Toledo, OH, USA
20/10/1977	Horton Fieldhouse, Illinois State University, Normal, IL, USA
21/10/1977	Bowen Fieldhouse, Eastern Michigan University, Ypsilanti, MI, USA
22/10/1977	Cole Field House, University of Maryland, College Park, MD, USA
23/10/1977	Hara Arena, Dayton, OH, USA
25/10/1977	Coliseum, Jackson, MS, USA
27/10/1977	Myriad Convention Centre, Oklahoma City, OK, USA
28/10/1977	Tarrant County Convention Centre, Fort Worth, TX, USA
29/10/1977	Assembly Centre, Louisiana State University, Baton Rouge, LA, USA
30/10/1977	Municipal Auditorium, Mobile, AL, USA
31/10/1977	Sam Houston Coliseum, Houston, TX, USA
1/11/1977	Sam Houston Coliseum, Houston, TX, USA
3/11/1977	Municipal Auditorium, Austin, TX, USA
4/11/1977	Barton Coliseum, Little Rock, AR, USA
5/11/1977	Hammons Centre, Springfield, MO, USA
7/11/1977	Duluth Arena, Duluth, MN, USA
8/11/1977	Dane County Coliseum, Madison, WI, USA
9/11/1977	Brown County Veteran's Memorial Arena, Green Bay, WI, USA
11/11/1977	Auditorium Arena, Omaha, NE, USA
12/11/1977	Ahearn Fieldhouse, Kansas State University, Manhattan, KS, USA
13/11/1977	Henry Levitt Arena, Wichita, KS, USA
15/11/1977	Jenison Fieldhouse, Michigan State University, Lansing, MI, USA
16/11/1977	Hall of Music, Purdue University, West Lafayette, IN, USA
18/11/1977	Civic Centre, Wheeling, WV, USA
20/11/1977	Mid-South Coliseum, Memphis, TN, USA
21/11/1977	Roberts Stadium, Evansville, IN, USA
22/11/1977	Von Braun Civic Centre Arena, Huntsville, AL, USA
24/11/1977	Coliseum, Macon, GA, USA
25/11/1977	Veterans Memorial Coliseum, Jacksonville, FL, USA
26/11/1977	Sportatorium, Hollywood, FL, USA
27/11/1977	Bayfront Centre, St Petersburg, FL, USA
30/11/1977	Veterans Memorial Coliseum, New Haven, CT, USA
23/12/1977	Earl's Court, London, England*
24/12/1977	Earl's Court, London, England*
26/12/1977	Earl's Court, London, England*
27/12/1977	Earl's Court, London, England*

*Shows thought to have been proposed but never took place.

16/1/1978	Montreal Forum, Montreal, QC, Canada
17/1/1978	Montreal Forum, Montreal, QC, Canada
18/1/1978	Kitchener Memorial Auditorium, Kitchener, ON, Canada
19/1/1978	Fairgrounds Coliseum, Columbus, OH, USA
20/1/1978	International Amphitheatre, Chicago, IL, USA

Tour Dates

21/1/1978	International Amphitheatre, Chicago, IL, USA
22/1/1978	International Amphitheatre, Chicago, IL, USA
24/1/1978	Hulman Civic University Centre, Terre Haute, IN, USA
25/1/1978	Richfield Coliseum, Richfield, OH, USA
26/1/1978	Coliseum, West Virginia University, Morgantown, WV, USA (rescheduled to 7/3)
27/1/1978	Riverfront Coliseum, Cincinnati, OH, USA (rescheduled to 8/3)
28/1/1978	Capital Centre, Landover, MD, USA
29/1/1978	Civic Centre, Springfield, MA, USA
30/1/1978	Barton Hall, Cornell University, Ithaca, NY, USA
1/2/1978	Memorial Auditorium, Buffalo, NY, USA
2/2/1978	Maple Leaf Gardens, Toronto, ON, Canada
3/2/1978	Maple Leaf Gardens, Toronto, ON, Canada
4/2/1978	Boston Garden, Boston, MA, USA
5/2/1978	The Spectrum, Philadelphia, PA, USA
6/2/1978	Field House, Rensselaer Polytechnic Institute, Troy, NY, USA
7/2/1978	Jadwin Gymnasium, Princeton University, Princeton, NJ, USA (rescheduled to 11/2)
8/2/1978	Field House, State University of New York, Plattsburgh, NY, USA
9/2/1978	Nassau Coliseum, Uniondale, NY, USA
10/2/1978	Nassau Coliseum, Uniondale, NY, USA
11/2/1978	Jadwin Gymnasium, Princeton University, Princeton, NJ, USA (rescheduled from 7/2)
12/2/1978	Onondaga County War Memorial, Syracuse, NY, USA
14/2/1978	Arena, Southern Illinois University, Carbondale, IL, USA
15/2/1978	Assembly Hall, University of Illinois, Champaign, IL, USA
16/2/1978	Western Hall, Western Illinois University, Macomb, IL, USA
18/2/1978	Coliseum, Stephen F. Austin State University, Nacogdoches, TX, USA
19/2/1978	Municipal Coliseum, Lubbock, TX, USA
20/2/1978	Ector County Coliseum, Odessa, TX, USA
21/2/1978	Fairgrounds Pavilion, Expo Square, Tulsa, OK, USA
22/2/1978	Civic Centre Coliseum, Amarillo, TX, USA
23/2/1978	County Coliseum, El Paso, TX, USA
24/2/1978	Activity Centre, Arizona State University, Tempe, AZ, USA
26/2/1978	Moby Gym, University of Colorado, Fort Collins, CO, USA
28/2/1978	Kemper Arena, Kansas City, MO, USA
1/3/1978	Checkerdome, St Louis, MO, USA
3/3/1978	Rupp Arena, Lexington, KY, USA
4/3/1978	Olympia Stadium, Detroit, MI, USA
6/3/1978	New Haven Coliseum, New Haven, CT, USA
7/3/1978	Coliseum, West Virginia University, Morgantown, WV, USA (rescheduled from 26/1)
8/3/1978	Riverfront Coliseum, Cincinnati, OH, USA (rescheduled from 27/1)
9/3/1978	The Omni, Atlanta, GA, USA
10/3/1978	Freedom Hall, Johnson City, TN, USA
12/3/1978	Civic Centre, Springfield, MA, USA
13/3/1978	Civic Centre, Providence, RI, USA
12/7/1987	Out In The Green Festival, Frauenfeld, Switzerland (cancelled due to Keith's wrist injury)
18/7/1987	Out In The Green Festival, Paderborn, Germany (cancelled due to Keith's wrist injury)
19/7/1987	Out In The Green Festival, St Wendel, Germany (cancelled due to Keith's wrist injury)
?/7/1992	Tower Theatre, Upper Darby, PA, USA (rehearsal)
21/7/1992	Tower Theatre, Upper Darby, PA, USA (rehearsal)
22/7/1992	Tower Theatre, Upper Darby, PA, USA (press/media preview show)
24/7/1992	Mann Music Centre, Philadelphia, PA, USA
25/7/1992	Jones Beach Theatre, Wantagh, NY, USA
26/7/1992	Garden State Centre, Holmdel, NJ, USA
28/7/1992	Merriweather Post Pavilion, Columbia, MD, USA
29/7/1992	Great Woods, Mansfield, MA, USA
31/7/1992	Waterloo Village, Stanhope, NJ, USA (radio broadcast)
1/8/1992	New York State Fairgrounds, Syracuse, NY, USA
2/8/1992	Palace Theatre, Albany, NY, USA

The ELP Story - *A Time and a Place*

4/8/1992	Bushnell Auditorium, Hartford, CT, USA
5/8/1992	L'agora Du Vieux-Port, Quebec City, QC, Canada
7/8/1992	Montreal Forum, Montreal, QC, Canada
8/8/1992	Finger Lakes Performing Arts Centre, Rochester, NY, USA
9/8/1992	Kingswood Music Centre, Toronto, ON, Canada
11/8/1992	Nautica Stage, Cleveland, OH, USA
12/8/1992	Pine Knob Music Theatre, Clarkston, MI, USA
13/8/1992	Riverbend Amphitheatre, Cincinnati, OH, USA
15/8/1992	Riverport Amphitheatre, St Louis, MO, USA
16/8/1992	World Music Theatre, Chicago, IL, USA
17/8/1992	Deer Creek Music Centre, Noblesville, IN, USA
18/8/1992	Chastain Park, Atlanta, GA, USA
20/8/1992	Starplex Amphitheatre, Dallas, TX, USA
21/8/1992	Woodlands Pavilion, Houston, TX, USA
22/8/1992	Sunken Garden Theatre, San Antonio, TX, USA
24/8/1992	Desert Sky Pavillion, Phoenix, AZ, USA
26/8/1992	Open-Air Theatre, San Diego, CA, USA
28/8/1992	Universal Amphitheatre, Los Angeles, CA, USA
29/8/1992	UC Irvine Bren Centre, Irvine, CA, USA
30/8/1992	UNLV Thomas and Mack Centre, Las Vegas, NV, USA
1/9/1992	Cal Expo Amphitheatre, Sacramento, CA, USA
2/9/1992	Concord Pavillion, Concord, CA, USA
4/9/1992	Schnitzer Auditorium, Portland, OR, USA
5/9/1992	Gorge Amphitheatre, George, WA, USA
6/9/1992	Orpheum Theatre, Vancouver, BC, Canada
10/9/1992	Kyoikubunkakaikan, Kawasaki, Japan
11/9/1992	Koseinenkinkaikan, Tokyo, Japan
12/9/1992	Shi Kokaido, Nagoya, Japan
14/9/1992	Koseinenkinkaikan, Osaka, Japan
16/9/1992	Hitomikinekodo, Tokyo, Japan
17/9/1992	Shibuya Kokaido, Tokyo, Japan
18/9/1992	Shibuya Kokaido, Tokyo, Japan
19/9/1992	Shibuya Kokaido, Tokyo, Japan
26/9/1992	Arena Di Verona, Verona, Italy
29/9/1992	Sports Halle, Budapest, Hungary
2/10/1992	Royal Albert Hall, London, England
3/10/1992	Royal Albert Hall, London, England
6/10/1992	Jahrhunderthalle, Frankfurt, Germany (postponed, Keith ill)
7/10/1992	Huxley's Neue Welt, Berlin, Germany
8/10/1992	Kuppelsaal, Hanover, Germany
10/10/1992	Stadthalle, Vienna, Austria
11/10/1992	Stadthalle, Heidelberg, Germany
12/10/1992	Eulachalle, Winterthur, Switzerland
13/10/1992	Siegerlandhalle, Siegen, Germany
15/10/1992	Oberfrankenhalle, Bayreuth, Germany
16/10/1992	Eissporthalle, Frankfurt, Germany
17/10/1992	E-Werk, Koln, Germany
18/10/1992	Grugahalle, Essen, Germany
20/10/1992	Philarmonie, Munich, Germany
21/10/1992	Jahrhunderthalle, Frankfurt, Germany (postponed again, Greg ill)
23/10/1992	Congresgebouw, The Hague, Holland (rescheduled to 7/11?)
25/10/1992	Apollo, Manchester, England
26/10/1992	Royal Albert Hall, London, England
28/10/1992	Kongresszentrum, Stuttgart, Germany
31/10/1992	Cuartel Conde Douque, Madrid, Spain
2/11/1992	Arena, Valencia, Spain
3/11/1992	Palais De Los Deportes, Barcelona, Spain
5/11/1992	Elisee Monmarte, Paris, France
6/11/1992	Forest National, Brussels, Belgium

Tour Dates

7/11/1992   Congresgebouw, The Hague, Holland
8/11/1992   Falkoner Theatre, Copenhagen, Denmark
10/11/1992 Centrum, Oslo, Norway
11/11/1992 Konserthuset, Stockholm, Sweden
14/11/1992 Donauhalle, Ulm, Germany
15/11/1992 Kulturpalast, Dresden, Germany
16/11/1992 Palaverde, Treviso, Italy (moved from Udine to Treviso)
17/11/1992 Palasport, Torino, Italy
19/11/1992 Palasport, Modena, Italy
20/11/1992 Palaghiaccio, Rome, Italy
21/11/1992 Palatrussardi, Milano, Italy
23/11/1992 Stadthalle, Freiburg, Germany
25/11/1992 International Centre, Bournemouth, England
26/11/1992 City Hall, Newcastle, England
27/11/1992 Symphony Hall, Birmingham, England
28/11/1992 Colston Hall, Bristol, England
30/11/1992 Kongresshalle, Frankfurt, Germany
1/12/1992   Congress Centrum, Hamburg, Germany

13/1/1993   North Alberta Jubilee Auditorium, Edmonton, AB, Canada
14/1/1993   South Alberta Jubilee Auditorium, Calgary, AB, Canada
15/1/1993   Centre Of The Arts, Regina, SAS, Canada
16/1/1993   Walker Theatre, Winnipeg, MAN, Canada
18/1/1993   Community Auditorium, Thunder Bay, ON, Canada
19/1/1993   Sudbury Arena, Sudbury, ON, Canada
20/1/1993   Centennial Hall, London, ON, Canada
21/1/1993   Congress Centre, Ottawa, ON, Canada
22/1/1993   Massey Hall, Toronto, ON, Canada
23/1/1993   Massey Hall, Toronto, ON, Canada
25/1/1993   Theatre St Denis, Montreal, QC, Canada
26/1/1993   Salle Albert Rousseau, Sainte-Foy, QC, Canada
28/1/1993   Memorial Auditorium, Burlington, VT, USA
29/1/1993   Orpheum Theatre, Boston, MA, USA
30/1/1993   Performing Arts Centre, Providence, RI, USA
1/2/1993   Paramount Theatre, Springfield, MA, USA
3/2/1993   Radio City Music Hall, New York, NY, USA
4/2/1993   Radio City Music Hall, New York, NY, USA
5/2/1993   Tower Theatre, Upper Darby, PA, USA
6/2/1993   Symphony Hall, Allentown, PA, USA
8/2/1993   A.J. Palumbo Theatre, Pittsburgh, PA, USA
9/2/1993   Palace Theatre, New Haven, CT, USA
10/2/1993   Mid-Hudson Civic Centre, Poughkeepsie, NY, USA
12/2/1993   Palace Theatre, Cleveland, OH, USA
13/2/1993   Veterans Memorial Auditorium, Columbus, OH, USA
15/2/1993   De Vos Hall at Grand Centre, Grand Rapids, MI, USA
16/2/1993   Ervin J. Nutter Centre, Dayton, OH, USA
17/2/1993   Fox Theatre, Detroit, MI, USA
19/2/1993   Northrup Theatre, Minneapolis, MN, USA
20/2/1993   Riverside Theatre, Milwaukee, WI, USA
21/2/1993   Chicago Theatre, Chicago, IL, USA
23/2/1993   Masonic Auditorium, Toledo, OH, USA
24/2/1993   Civic Centre Theatre, Madison, WI, USA
26/2/1993   Adler Theatre, Davenport, IA, USA
27/2/1993   Stephens Auditorium, Ames, IA, USA
28/2/1993   Peoria Civic Centre, Peoria, IL, USA
2/3/1993   Music Hall, Omaha, NE, USA
3/3/1993   Midland Theatre, Kansas City, MO, USA
4/3/1993   Brady Theatre, Tulsa, OK, USA
5/3/1993   Coliseum, Denver, CO, USA (cancelled)

The ELP Story - *A Time and a Place*

6/3/1993   Kiva Auditorium, Albuquerque, NM, USA
9/3/1993   BSU Pavillion Arena, Boise, ID, USA
10/3/1993 Kindsbury Hall, University of Utah, Salt Lake City, UT, USA
12/3/1993 Pioneer Theatre, Reno, NV, USA
13/3/1993 Warnors Theatre, Fresno, CA, USA
14/3/1993 Warfield Theatre, San Francisco, CA, USA
16/3/1993 Wiltern Theatre, Los Angeles, CA, USA
17/3/1993 Wiltern Theatre, Los Angeles, CA, USA
19/3/1993 Auditorio Nacional, Mexico City, Mexico
20/3/1993 Auditorio Nacional, Mexico City, Mexico
24/3/1993 Canecao, Rio De Janeiro, Brazil
25/3/1993 Palace, Sao Paulo, Brazil
26/3/1993 Palace, Sao Paulo, Brazil
27/3/1993 Palace, Sao Paulo, Brazil
31/3/1993 Estadio Chile, Santiago, Chile
1/4/1993   Estadio Chile, Santiago, Chile
3/4/1993   Estadio De Obras Sanitarias, Buenos Aires, Argentina
4/4/1993   Estadio De Obras Sanitarias, Buenos Aires, Argentina
5/4/1993   Estadio De Obras Sanitarias, Buenos Aires, Argentina
17/11/1993 Beacon Theatre, New York, NY, USA (Hungerthon benefit)
23/11/1993 Virgin Record Store, Los Angeles, CA, USA
17/12/1993 Hollywood Palladium, Hollywood, CA, USA

(Opening for Jethro Tull 18/8 to 29/9/96)

18/8/1996 Darien Lake Theme Park, Darien Centre, NY, USA
19/8/1996 Kingswood Music Theatre, Toronto, ON, Canada
21/8/1996 Montage Mountain, Scranton, PA, USA
22/8/1996 PNC Bank Arts Centre, Holmdel, NJ, USA
23/8/1996 Merriweather Post Pavillion, Columbia, MD, USA
25/8/1996 Meadows Music Theatre, Hartford, CT, USA
26/8/1996 Great Woods Centre, Mansfield, MA, USA
27/8/1996 New York State Fairgrounds, Syracuse, NY, USA
29/8/1996 Star Pavillion, Hershey, PA, USA
30/8/1996 Jones Beach Theatre, Wantagh, NY, USA
31/8/1996 Sony Music Entertainment Centre, Camden, NJ, USA
1/9/1996   Riverplex Amphitheatre, Pittsburgh, PA, USA
3/9/1996   Nautica Stage, Cleveland, OH, USA
4/9/1996   Polaris Amphitheatre, Columbus, OH, USA
5/9/1996   Pine Knob Music Theatre, Clarkston, MI, USA
6/9/1996   Riverbend Music Centre, Cincinnati, OH, USA
7/9/1996   World Music Theatre, Tinley Park, IL, USA
8/9/1996   Mark Of The Quad Cities, Moline, IL, USA
10/9/1996 Northrup Auditorium, Minneapolis, MN, USA
11/9/1996 Marcus Amphitheatre, Milwaukee, WI, USA
13/9/1996 Riverport Amphitheatre, St Louis, MO, USA
14/9/1996 Sandstone Amphitheatre, Bonner Springs, KS, USA
15/9/1996 Civic Auditorium Arena, Omaha, NE, USA
16/9/1996 Fiddlers Green Amphitheatre, Englewood, CO, USA (cancelled)
18/9/1996 Desert Sky Pavillion, Phoenix, AZ, USA
19/9/1996 Aladdin Theatre, Las Vegas, NV, USA
20/9/1996 Open-Air Theatre, San Diego, CA, USA
21/9/1996 Irvine Meadows, Irvine, CA, USA
22/9/1996 Universal Amphitheatre, Los Angeles, CA, USA
24/9/1996 Concord Pavillion, Concord, CA, USA
25/9/1996 Reno Amphitheatre, Reno, NV, USA
27/9/1996 Gorge Amphitheatre, George, WA, USA
28/9/1996 Labor Day Amphitheatre, Salem, OR, USA

Tour Dates

29/9/1996	BSU Pavillion, Boise, ID, USA
8/10/1996	Sun Palace, Fukuoka, Japan
9/10/1996	Festival Hall, Osaka, Japan
10/10/1996	Shi Kokaido, Nagoya, Japan
12/10/1996	Shibuya Kokaido, Tokyo, Japan
13/10/1996	Koseinenkin Hall, Tokyo, Japan
14/10/1996	Izumi T-2, Sendai, Japan
15/10/1996	Sun Plaza, Tokyo, Japan
17/10/1996	Sun Plaza, Tokyo, Japan
18/10/1996	Sun Plaza, Tokyo, Japan
19/10/1996	Bunka Centre, Saitama Urawa, Japan
12/6/1997	The Joint-Hard Rock Café, Las Vegas, NV, USA
16/6/1997	Lakewood Amphitheatre, Atlanta, GA, USA
20/6/1997	Kissstadion, Budapest, Hungary
22/6/1997	Spodek, Katowice, Poland
23/6/1997	Palace Of Culture, Prague, Czechoslovakia
24/6/1997	Tollwood, Munich, Germany
26/6/1997	Patinore De Kockelschuer, Petange, Luxembourg
28/6/1997	Stadthalle, Kassel, Germany
29/6/1997	Paradiso, Amsterdam, Holland
1/7/1997	Serandadenhof Atrium, Nurnberg, Germany
2/7/1997	Elysee Montmartre, Paris, France
4/7/1997	Peisnitzinsel, Halle, Germany (Out In The Green Festival)
5/7/1997	Westfalenpark, Dortmund, Germany (Out In The Green Festival)
6/7/1997	Lahr Airfield, Lahr, Germany (Daytona Festival)
7/7/1997	Auditorium Stravinski, Montreux, Switzerland (Montreux Festival)
11/7/1997	Museumshof, Fulda, Germany
12/7/1997	Grosse Freiheit, Hamburg, Germany
13/7/1997	Elbufer, Dresden, Germany
18/7/1997	Velodromo, Quartu, Italy
20/7/1997	Piazza Olimpo, Stiviere, Italy
21/7/1997	Centralino Del Foro Italico, Rome, Italy
25/7/1997	Villaggio Della Musica, Bellinzona, Switzerland (Kingdom Festival)
6/8/1997	Teatro Guaira, Curitiba, Brazil
8/8/1997	Gran Rex, Buenos Aires, Argentina
9/8/1997	Gran Rex, Buenos Aires, Argentina
10/8/1997	Avenida Das Hortensias, Gramado, Brazil
12/8/1997	Estadio Chile, Santiago, Chile
13/8/1997	Estadio Chile, Santiago, Chile
15/8/1997	Mineirinho Gymnasium, Belo Horizonte, Brazil
16/8/1997	Metropolitan, Rio De Janeiro, Brazil
18/8/1997	Olympia, Sao Paulo, Brazil
19/8/1997	Olympia, Sao Paulo, Brazil
20/8/1997	Olympia, Sao Paulo, Brazil
21/8/1997	Gran Rex, Buenos Aires, Argentina
6/9/1997	Wolf Trap, Vienna, VA, USA
7/9/1997	Oakdale Theatre, Wallingford, CT, USA
8/9/1997	State Theatre, New Brunswick, NJ, USA
10/9/1997	Beacon Theatre, New York, NY, USA
11/9/1997	Tower Theatre, Upper Darby, PA, USA
12/9/1997	Harborlights, Boston, MA, USA
13/9/1997	Sands Hotel and Casino, Atlantic City, NJ, USA
14/9/1997	Westbury Music Fair, Westbury, NY, USA
17/9/1997	Nautica Stage, Cleveland, OH, USA
18/9/1997	The Palace, Auburn Hills, MI, USA
19/9/1997	Rosemont Theatre, Rosemont, IL, USA
20/9/1997	Riverside Theatre, Milwaukee, WI, USA

The ELP Story - *A Time and a Place*

21/9/1997   Fox Theatre, St Louis, MO, USA
23/9/1997   Union Hall, Phoenix, AZ, USA
25/9/1997   Universal Amphitheatre, Los Angeles, CA, USA
26/9/1997   Concord Pavilion, Concord, CA, USA
27/9/1997   Reno Amphitheatre, Reno, NV, USA
28/9/1997   Concert Centre, Visalia, CA, USA
30/9/1997   Humphrey's By The Bay, San Diego, CA, USA
4/10/1997   Muello Uno Teatro, Lima, Peru
7/10/1997   Teatro Nacional, San Jose, Costa Rica (cancelled?)
8/10/1997   Teatro Nacional, San Jose, Costa Rica
10/10/1997   Plaza De Toros, Monterrey, Mexico (cancelled)
11/10/1997   Teatro Cine Opera, Mexico City, Mexico
12/10/1997   Teatro Cine Opera, Mexico City, Mexico (cancelled)

(Opening for Deep Purple and Dream Theater 6/8 to 30/8/98)

1/8/1998   Casino Ballroom, Hampton Beach, NH, USA
2/8/1998   Flynn Theatre, Burlington, VT, USA
3/8/1998   The Chance, Poughkeepsie, NY, USA
4/8/1998   Cumberland County Civic Centre, Portland, ME, USA (cancelled)
6/8/1998   PNC Bank Arts Centre, Holmdel, NJ, USA
7/8/1998   Meadows Music Theatre, Hartford, CT, USA
8/8/1998   Great Woods, Mansfield, MA, USA
9/8/1998   Jones Beach Theatre, Wantagh, NY, USA
11/8/1998   Bud Light Amphitheatre, Harvey's Lake, PA, USA
12/8/1998   Blockbuster Entertainment Centre, Camden, NJ, USA (cancelled)
14/8/1998   Finger Lakes Performing Arts Centre, Canandaigua, NY, USA
15/8/1998   Pine Knob Music Theatre, Clarkston, MI, USA
17/8/1998   L'agora Vieux De Port, Quebec City, QC, Canada
18/8/1998   Molson Centre, Montreal, QC, Canada
19/8/1998   Molson Amphitheatre, Toronto, ON, Canada
21/8/1998   Blossom Music Centre, Cuyahoga Falls, OH, USA
22/8/1998   World Music Centre, Tinley Park, IL, USA
23/8/1998   Grand Casino Amphitheatre, Hinkley, MN, USA
24/8/1998   Marcus Amphitheatre, Milwaukee, WI, USA
26/8/1998   Fiddler's Green Amphitheatre, Greenwood Village, CO, USA
28/8/1998   Warfield Theatre, San Francisco, CA, USA
29/8/1998   Warfield Theatre, San Francisco, CA, USA (cancelled)
29/8/1998   The Joint-Hard Rock Café, Las Vegas, NV, USA
30/8/1998   Universal Amphitheatre, Los Angeles, CA, USA
31/8/1998   4th and B, San Diego, CA, USA

25/7/2010   Victoria Park, London, England (High Voltage Festival)